Generation whY?
Everything You Should Know About What Young People Think

Generation whY?

Everything You Should Know About What Young People Think

by
Kevin Jordan

Table of Contents

To My Grandparents
For doing all that you and your generation has done to
allow my generation to do.

To My Parents
For giving me, and always listening to my voice. I know
I always have an audience with you.

"[Y]ours has become a generation possessed with that most American of ideas: that people who love their country can change it for the better."
- President Barack Obama

Chapter 0:
If I Named it the "Preface" You Wouldn't Read It

Understand that this is a critique of Generation Y, just as much as it is a criticism of other generation's acceptance or lack of acceptance for this generation's ideas. Generations before ours operate under a guise that young people should be more involved in society, but really they want young people to speak without being heard. To be fair, the blame ultimately falls on Generation Y for not asking why. Why are we not given an equal say in issues that matter to us most. Why are older people the ones making decisions that affect us, yet we have no say at all?

We are the generation that introduced Facebook to the world, and whether or not that is something to be proud of, what we really have to analyze is what are American young people doing with these tools to effect real change? This is not a manifesto for a generation, but rather a plea for people to think critically about where we can go from here. I wrote this because I do not so much fear for the future of this generation, as I do fear the way older people continuously pigeonhole us into what we are not. Out of sheer frustration I wrote what would not suffice in a tweet, a Facebook status or a single blog post. I used a medium that has a proven record and is still considered "legitimate," or at least for the time being. There is more that needs to be said than is probably covered in this book, and it should be said more often. Young people in this country are not voiceless, but they have been put on mute. We have a couple of choices when it comes to this issue. We can do nothing about it and wait until we are older, or we can take action now to right the wrongs of our generation and those that preceded ours.

At times you will see the word "I" in this book. It has been a matter of common opinion in my education that a person should never use the word "I" in writing because it dilutes the argument. It puts personal opinion ahead of the opinion. However, in a book like this it is important to understand that young people have opinions too. When we try to put our voices in with the masses, those with "more experience" drown us out. Just because you have a mouth does not mean you have to voice your opinion, but when young people are not heard, a perspective that is like no other group of people is completely ignored. I have been blamed for things because of my age and I have been praised because of my age. It has been a factor that has caused people to doubt what I can do, and it has even been a means for people to blame their own shortcomings on me. Since age is something I cannot control, it has nothing to do with my successes and failures. This is what most people, regardless of their own age fail to remember. Age is not synonymous with maturity. Older people will think and argue otherwise, but that is because they are older. The one thing that they have over us younger people is age and they will always win in that category. Although this is not a competition, it is very much a zero sum game where the preponderance of the power is shifted toward one end of the spectrum – the spectrum that has more grey hairs.

This is the biggest disclaimer and it is written mostly to ward off criticism because I already know what is going to be said. The claims in this book do not suggest that all young people think one way or another. It does not imply that all young people are inactive in politics or do not try to enact social change. I know environmentalists fighting for the planet, activists seeking equality for gender issues and LGBT rights, and future politicians of this country who want to make the world a better place. I am only suggesting that no matter how small a minority it is, it is a minority. This should not offend any young person who is actually doing his or her part. I am on your side and want more people like you.

More importantly to anyone who would no longer consider himself or herself a young person, this book does not pit one generation against another. Some of the criticisms often said against young people, you can blame older for as well. Conversely, things that young people can celebrate and declare victories for, older people have a hand in as well and are just as responsible for their successes. The real premise that must be understood is that Generation Y is one that needs to learn from, improve upon, and do things better than the generations before us. It is not a competition that we are trying to win. We are merely trying to advance this country and improve it in every way possible. You should want the same for us.

The last caveat that I must make is I understand that this is a global generation, probably more than ever before because of social media. That being said, the reason I chose to focus on America is not just because I live in this country. It is because we have a responsibility to help ourselves just as much as we try to help others in need beyond these borders. There are horrendous problems all over the world. We should attend to these issues, but we cannot forget about what is going on in America as a consequence of having a global conscious.

There are going to have to be advocates in this country pushing for social change here at home.

There will be grammatical errors throughout this book, but thus is the life of a self-publishing writer. There will also be parts that you may disagree with, but thus is the life of a human being. Somehow trivialities like a misplaced comma often distract us, or we get so stubborn with our ideas that we refuse to listen to a viewpoint that we do not agree with. This was written out of frustration, in times of happiness, quickly, slowly, labouringly and sometimes out of pure enjoyment. There were parts I feared writing. There were parts I feared other people reading. There were other parts I felt too strongly about to not want to include. There were many emotions put into it, but that is not the intention I had in writing it. The intention I have is to provide something where others can get something out of it.

It is also my every intention to be fair in my statements of any political parties, ideas, and beliefs. No opinion expressed here is to align with a political agenda, and the fact that I even need to say this reveals a fundamental problem that this country has with a lack of trust in one another's opinions. Everyone thinks that everyone else is out to serve some political end and get a partisan agenda across. As an English major the first rule of any reader is to bypass the author's intent in order to dig deeper than what is on the page, but I am delivering my intent to you as clearly as possible. My intent is that I have none at all. Forget everything I said before. Why would I expect anyone to listen to what I have to say and actually care? I am not out to change anyone's mind or convince anyone of anything. But then again, I am just another kid from Generation Y.

Chapter 1:
What is Generation Y?

Generation Y is lazy and they don't work hard. Kids today don't care about the future of this country or this planet. The youth today have it so much easier than older generations. I have been on this planet for 22 years and I have heard the same inaccuracies thrown on my generation for 22 years. Listening to one's parents and grandparents before them allows one to get a sense of where they came from and who they are. This is undisputed. We should celebrate their triumphs, acknowledge their pains, understand their viewpoints, but we cannot hold onto the same perspectives they had growing up and try to apply them to the world we live in today. 1960 looks a lot different than 2013 and that is for better and worse.

I am not all that interested in when Generation Y started, or if and when it ended. I am more interested in what legacy this generation will leave behind and how we will be described. Generation Y is the millennial generation that no longer has to go to the library for research, walk down the street to talk to a friend, or buy music. Generation Y does not go outside, but instead builds virtual worlds where we can explore the entire world on a computer screen. Generation Y does not play sports outdoors, but uses a controller in place of a bat and enters the major leagues from our living rooms. There is a culture difference where we are becoming homebodies that do not venture out beyond our doors because that world can be accessed from an iPhone.

Because generation Z has not yet been named, it is not

11

too late to change the characteristics of a people that can leave a legacy behind bigger than the invention of social networks. Everyday from every living older person we hear that it is up to this generation to take a stand and help improve the course that this country is on. We must participate and get involved in politics, society and our communities to protect the future of this country and this planet. It is our responsibility and we have the ability to enact real change. Sounds great. The problem is, the same people who say these things are the ones who are not doing it themselves. Politicians are the ones in power right now and they are the ones who can make actual changes. We are all going to have to take responsibility for what we all can do. Generation Y is not alone in the fight for a better country, but that also means we have to join the fight.

Generation Y has been credited and shamed with the idea that we are selfish and narcissistic. Selfish I can clearly understand, as everything in our world is personalized and customized. Gone is the one-size-fits all style of living because now there is an entitlement that we have that everything must be catered to the individual. With improvements in technology we have learned to expect our everyday lives to be delivered to us in a package with our name on it. Everything is personalized from movie recommendations, shopping experiences, news feeds and anything else that can be accessed through technology. This is really no fault of our own, as consumers demand a certain level of personal touch to the products they buy so companies fulfill the orders. We have gotten to a point in our lives where our imaginations cannot keep up with the technology. That is the essence of Generation Y. We build things bigger and better than anyone could ever imagine. Creating things "just for me" has become the framework for people who want to keep up with technology.

Although I understand the selfish nature of this generation, I do not understand the narcissism. What do we have to be narcissistic about? I am not one of those doom and gloom people that cannot find the good in what we do, but in what will follow in the rest of this chapter and this book, as I hope you will see, there is so much more that we could be doing than building gadgets. What do we have to brag about? The minute people start bragging is the moment they have given up on making progress. They have stopped moving forward to reflect on the accomplishments they achieved, only to bolster their own ego. History will tell our story, but we spend so much time trying to get our names in the book that we don't make actual contributions that this society needs to be great. Everyone wants to be the young billionaire not knowing how to get there. Everyone wants to be the next Mark Zuckerberg not wanting to work to get there. There is no direct path to get "there," but as long as there are still inequalities and injustices in this country, we will never get "there."

Generation Y is the misguided and unguided band of individuals who have a severe need to become individuals. There is this recurring idea that runs throughout this generation that each and every person should be unique. Never before has the idea of individuality been marketed so heavily, but this kind of individualism and ego boosting is driving a wedge between young people and change. Instead of wanting to change the world, they merely want to change themselves and look as different as they can from the other people like them. There is a constant desire to set oneself apart from everyone else and in order to do this, you have to focus on the differences. This might be okay when a person is looking for a job or trying to pop out in a stack of resumes, but for the future of this country, we are going to have to unite at some point.

This generation has more opportunities and tools at our disposal than any other generation before us. The only problem is there are really two paths that we can take. We can use the information and technology that we have for social good or for our own personal good. What many fail to realize is that the former includes the latter. If society prevails, than all of us individuals prevail. When the economy succeeds, businesses succeed so then people succeed. This is not a trickle down theory on social action because we all know that voodoo economics does not work. The reason why this is not top down economics is because it ultimately starts with the individual. No one from above is going to just give power to someone below, let alone a 20-year-old. People are going to have to start vying for their own power and creating change when they can, themselves.

It is almost impossible to characterize an entire generation. I tried to do that in the over-generalizing characteristics I mentioned above. The only factor that we should really consider is the fact that Generation Y is not considered over. Since it is not over, we are going to need help in making the changes we all want possible. This is where the generation of baby boomers and Generation X come in. It is not so much that we need their help, as we need them to just allow us to join them. The participation we need from Generation X in our fight for change is for them to be willing to stand side by side along our generation and acknowledge our voices.

The reason why people have such problems with young people is age. It is not always the age itself, but what people can interpret from it. They begin to associate a number with many other character attributes, and the most common misnomer is that age has a direct relationship to maturity. A person can be 50 years old and never really grow up, but the 50-year-old person will definitely be quicker to get a promotion than his or her younger cohorts. I am sure people will say that age might not be directly related to maturity, but it has a relationship to experience. This is also not necessarily the case because a young person is not unknowledgeable or inexperienced by default. Older people might have more experience working with something, but that does not mean they will offer new and fresh approaches. Whereas inexperience might hinder young people from having a complete understanding of something, complacency is a poison just as evil to older people who get caught in a rut of offering the same old ideas to new problems. Young and new ideas are exactly what young people have to offer, yet somehow the qualities we cherish are the ones you have to develop with time. Forget what is best because we just stick to what is oldest because we are comfortable with that. The young people of this generation are not going to wait for older people to figure out that their ideas are sometimes outdated. That is why there are so many startups springing up all over the Silicon Valley. Generation Y will not let age become a great excuse for older people to bypass us for promotions, treat us with little respect and ignore us altogether. We will just start our own company and circumvent any problems we might encounter in a corporation run by old people.

This is a beautiful quality and also a dreadful flaw in our generation. We will go out of our way to avoid trouble. We will do anything and everything that we can to avoid the problems that have hindered our society for ages. We will build and create new products that revolutionize industries and we are constantly trying to make life more comfortable for people. We might have the voracity to start our own company and solve technical and technological problems, but we are not bold enough to collectively unite and fight the wrongs in our world head on.

What we seem unwilling to do is actually do something that requires more than a computer to fix. Revolutions did not happen with mobile phones or tablets. People used to become inspired and motivated simply by an idea of equality, but young people have lost that visionary thinking in this country that usually and historically resulted in actual action. Instead we see a problem and think how we can profit monetarily, instead of socially. As progressive as this generation is credited with being in our ideas, you would think we would take those opinions and make something of them. For us, opinions often just remain opinions. Unfortunately though, for us, inaction breeds inaction, and we have yet to learn actions warrant reactions. The reaction we receive may not always be the one we want, but without making a stand, people will continue to ignore us. We will not always get the progress we are looking for and at times it will feel like a losing battle. Nonetheless, without actually verbalizing the opinions we have, we will never enact change.

This generation is not a generation that will sit idly by and hope that things will get better on their own. Since older people are willing to pass the torch (eventually) in terms of giving young people a chance to speak, then we must be willing to take it. If it is a generation that thinks progress is made without people getting involved, then everything that the older people say about us is justified and true. If we are not willing to fight for what we believe in then we might as well stop believing altogether because what is the point otherwise?

As I said before, it is up to this generation to do all that it can to bring about the changes we want to see. If we are going to claim defeat before we have even start the battle then we might as well settle for the idea that the way things are is as good as it is going to get. There will still forever be inequality among races, classes, religions, sexualities, and belief systems. There will forever be a widening gap between the rich and the poor. We will never address the poverty issues. We will not decrease the deficit. We will not create jobs for Americans wanting to work. Immigration reform will never happen. The planet will continue to get polluted and animals will continue to go extinct. Climate change will continue to persist and this planet will soon be uninhabitable. Healthcare will never be available to every person in this country. Senseless mass killings will still take the lives of innocent people. We will enter into wars we do not believe in. We will continue to allow other countries with an agenda to attack us. We will not fight terrorism. We will not prevent dangerous countries from acquiring nuclear weapons. If you think that there is nothing to be done then old people might be right in thinking that above every other way to describe Generation Y, the best way to characterize this generation is to say that it is doomed.

Chapter 2:
Social Media Has Made Us Less Social

The crowning glory of our generation is social media. Despite this, social media could be the heart of many of our problems. I am not going to take a typical stance about how social media has plagued our generation to being lazy because we don't talk anymore. This is an all too common conversation. Texting, status updates, and tweets may have ruined face-to-face interactions, but that is not a debate I find valuable. One that needs to be had more is what social media has done for our desire to promote social action. Instead of protests and sit-ins, people change their profile pictures on Facebook to show their support of some political or social movement taking place at the time. Essentially, we can become social activists without ever leaving our couches.

Knowledge is power, but sometimes power is power. Everyone loves to tout how social media played a huge role in the Arab Spring, and we have to acknowledge that information can be spread to ends of the earth that will bring light to the people fighting in shadows. We are certainly more aware of issues that we may have never known about before, but knowing that injustices occur and not acting on them makes us somewhat complicit in the atrocities happening to people all over the world and to the injustices happening in our own country. Changing your picture on Facebook for a month or a week is a nice gesture, but what changed? Knowledge is only power when it is used for good and to act upon what you know.

Social media has made us desensitized to issues like war, revolutions, killings, murders, suicides, terrorism and others because we see them, we hear about them, and yet all we do is send out a tweet. Instead of using this "power" in the form of knowledge to write congress to take action, take action ourselves, or fight for our own rights in our own country, we become cynics of what will actually change. We take to these social media outlets complaining about the government who does nothing, as we sit and do nothing ourselves. We have become desensitized because we get information instantaneously and we can find out anything we want in seconds. Therefore, gruesome images, troubling information and videos are all at our fingertips. We don't have to witness these things firsthand, nor are they shocking anymore because we see them on a computer screen, protected by complete anonymity, everyday.

Think about the issues in the United States that people are fighting everyday. Racism, LGBT (lesbian, gay, bi-sexual, transgender) rights, women's rights, and ageism, is a short list of social challenges this nation faces. I see people post updates on different social networks everyday about how this nation should be better, think better, and do better, yet they do nothing about it other than complain. I do not want to criticize or attack those that are actually trying to make a difference in this world because those people do exist. However they are a minority that gets drowned out by the noise and distractions occupying our time and thoughts.

This brings me to the biggest point I can make in criticism against social media. Think about the great orators and people that have actually made a difference in this world, and I am willing to guess that none of them come from Generation Y, or even lived in the past 30 years. Did Barack Obama come to mind? I will discuss the impact President Obama *could have* had later in this book, so do not worry, but I would not put him in this category yet. One of the most recognized orators who actually changed something in this country is Martin Luther King Jr. MLK is often an overused example, but there is nothing more fitting for this particular example because he did not have Facebook, Twitter, or Instagram. What he did have was a voice that could rally millions of people to unite for a common cause. He could get thousands of people to march in the streets and protest for what they believed in. We have the tools at our disposal that could be great rallying solutions and could help build up the voices of our generation. Yet, there has been no MLK, or person with the power to bring people together like him, since he died.

If Facebook had existed when MLK was around, would his voice have just gotten drowned out in the noise that fills the social networks? Would he have just been someone taking to twitter talking about change, but not moving these conversations to the streets? Of course we all know that he did not have these tools, nor could he speak to the masses in a way that we can on the Internet, and that is probably for the netter. He still goes down in history as one of the most powerful voices of any generation.

Think about the way these social networks are designed because they really are great equalizers. Interestingly enough the only equality we might have in this country is on social networks, but this is not what Martin Luther King was hoping for. When you sign up for an account everyone's profile looks exactly the same, you have no friends, you have no followers, and the profile is completely blank. Because of this, a future convict is given equal voice and place on these sites, as the next president of our nation. If Martin Luther King Jr. were around today, his words would be on the same page as a goat making human sounds.

The argument could be made that because of people like Martin Luther King Jr. we can enjoy more pleasures in life so there is less need for someone to be a voice of a generation. Although we have come a long way in terms of civil rights, there are still fights to be had and not just in terms of black and white relations. Now more than ever, we need people to rise up as leaders and fight for the changes in our country that we complain about on social networks. Technology and social media may have improved a lot of things, but in terms of social *action*, we have sacrificed authentic change for mass exploits of outward demonstrations.

Leave social media to the marketers and the people who like to think that it is going to lead to the next revolution. Make no mistake about it. It can be a very powerful tool in helping spread information, but it is not all that it is cracked up to be. Twitter and Facebook were helpful with the Arab Spring at first glance because many, even the Egyptian activists themselves suggest it mostly helped people outside of the revolting countries receive word of their actions more than it did people within them. Egyptian activists claim that social media did not power their revolution, as it was a grassroots movement.[1] Claiming that social media was the reason for their

---

[1] Lisa Goldman, "Social Media Has Been a Mixed Blessing for the Arab Spring," *Tech President,* http://techpresident.com/news/wegov/23510/social-media-harming-arab-uprising, accessed 2 May 2013.

unison is demeaning to the work they put in to unite.

What is the biggest piece of evidence that Twitter and Facebook were not the driving forces for a revolution in Egypt that everyone wanted them to be? During the five days of the Mubarak regime, the Internet and mobile phone networks were shut off. People did not even have Internet and social media to mobilize so they had to do it by word of mouth. So much for the power of social media. The only thing social media accomplished, as I said before, is that the rest of the world got to see what the activists were doing in real time. Despite previous myths about social media's powerful ways being dispelled, this seems like a good thing, right? Information like this should be spread all around the world. But the problem is the headlines get put on the wrong things. What do we focus on here in *their* story: social media. We take away the credit of activists fighting for something and doing so by traditional means, by giving credit to a tweet. We take away from their actual reasons for fighting and focus on something that does not even matter. What the people need is actual change and justice – not a follower on Twitter.

What most people say is the best part of social media could be crippling actual change. Everyone says that social media has power to reach everyone in real time, but because tons of information becomes proliferated into our news feeds, we might be reaching too far. Think about the way information used to be delivered and shared to people. There was a culture of everyone gathering around the radio or the television set when there were only three channels to choose from and all of them were news stations. Everyone got the same information, no matter if they wanted to hear it or not.

Now, people can choose from hundreds of channels, thousands of news websites, thousands of podcasts, and hundreds of other different media sources. I can tune into what I want, and completely turn off what I don't like. If I only want to hear about Kim Kardashian, I can personalize my preferences to only give me updates on her. I never have to listen to anything political or engage in conversations that may make me think differently about society than I already think. I get to live in my bubble forever. We have more information in front of us than ever before, but the ability to choose what we pay attention to has allowed us to only pick the sources that align with what we already believe.

In terms of political television today we have the big three: MSNBC, FOX News and CNN. Despite their mantras and attempts at remaining unbiased, they have their leanings. Fox is conservative, MSNBC is liberal, and CNN wants to deliver the news first despite being obligated to deliver facts. This is exactly why social media has created unrealistic expectations for the future of our country. Television came first, but these news channels are further evidence that people are only willing to listen to one side of arguments – the side they already agree with.

If we want an imbalance of liberal rhetoric than MSNBC is what you tune into. If you are an MSNBC loyalist and then only watch FOX to hear what the opposition is saying, you are not listening with both ears open. You are trying to figure out what the "enemy" is saying. The truth is, rarely is any person simply a liberal or simply a conservative. There are some issues that you can be progressive about and want to see changed, but there are others that you may think the government should have no hand in at all. Nonetheless, we pick a team anyway and then find the information that best supports our agendas. We are not interested in having our minds changed or become fully educated on a topic. We make up our minds, pick a team and only watch the channel that agrees with our philosophy. Then we go follow that one group on Twitter and only listen to their biased tweets.

Not only that, but we want information fast and because of that we sacrifice fact checking and credibility for instantaneous results. Not only do we find information tailored to what we already believe, but we also often get wrong information that only provides further evidence of our lack of desire to actually be informed. We merely have a desire to be right, or at least just find information that supports our claims. No one has to actually be objectively right or deliver the truth anymore. Since lies become proliferated across the Internet so quickly, it is impossible to pull them back once they have been distributed. This has led to cyber bullying, political and personal defamation and an outright propagation of lies.

Politicians are already seen as shady characters. However, with the invention of social media, there is really nothing the best PR team in the world could do to fix some of the accusations made against them today. The only thing they have going for them is that there are so many lies spread everyday that people become so baffled as to what they believe. If the given politician is on your team, you are more inclined to deny the lies, but if he or she is on the other team, then of course the person is a communist, anti-American propagandist looking to take over the country. Although I would like to say that these are made up, what follows below are actual quotes made about politicians in this country. You are going to have to consider the source with some of them, but they should still be pointed out:

1. In 2008 candidate Obama was accused of "palling around with terrorists" for his quasi relationship with William Ayers, who is now a professor at the University of Chicago.[2] Sarah Palin famously quipped this sound bite, wink and all, so like I said, consider the source.

2. In an interview, Ted Nugent had this to say about president Obama: "He is an evil, dangerous man who hates America and hates freedom."[3]

3. An official for President Obama, Stephanie Cutter, suggested that Mitt Romney committed a "felony" for his work at Bain capital, implying to the voting public that he should be in prison, rather than running for president.[4]

---

[2] CNN, "Fact Check: Is Obama 'palling around with terrorists'?", *CNN,* "http://politicalticker.blogs.cnn.com/2008/10/05/fact-check-is-obama-palling-around-with-terrorists/, accessed 3 May 2013

[3] The Huffington Post, "Ted Nugent Suggests He's Ready For Armed Revolt Against 'Evil, Dangerous' Obama," *The Huffington Post,* http://www.huffingtonpost.com/2013/01/22/ted-nugent-armed-revolt_n_2527608.html, date accessed 5 May 2013

[4] Fox News, "Presidential rivals trade charges of lying, Romney calls for apology over 'felony' remark," *Fox News,* http://www.foxnews.com/politics/2012/07/12/presidential-rivals-trade-charges-lying-romney-demands-apology-over-felony/, data accessed: 5 May 2013

4. In a presidential debate, President Obama claimed that Mitt Romney called the racist Arizona immigration law a "model for the nation."[5] Romney actually said the part of the law where employers could verify if a worker was here illegally or not was agreeable –not the entire law.

It is enough to merely suggest that someone has done something bad for it to be picked up by the mainstream media that the person actually did it. President Obama is a terrorist and Mitt Romney is a wanted criminal. Something so vile can be said without any bit of remorse and of course these are all protected by the first amendment, but when did a right to free speech become a way for people to merely say what they want without it being truthful? Everyone can have criticisms against our president, against Mitt Romney, or anyone else in the public eye, but when we are supposed to trust these people with our lives, we cannot have loose cannons firing off untruths and blatant misrepresentations. The rest of America demands the truth, but if they are fed lies, we have no choice but to eat it all up. What else do we have? The truth does not bring in ratings.

This is not only an issue with public figures. Cyber bullying has become a serious issue for this generation of young people. Over half of young people in this country have been bullied online, and close to the same number has done some form of cyber bullying. About a third of young people have been threatened online. If parents are reading this and think cyber bullying is not happening to

[5] Tampa Bay Times, "Barack Obama says Mitt Romney called the Arizona immigration law a 'model for the nation.'", *Tampa Bay Times,*

their children, half of those children that are bullied do not tell their parents.[6] Children are hurting and killing themselves because of messages are left for them online, and often shared with the rest of the world. We can say it is all fun and games when it comes to politicians and celebrities, although they are people too. Nevertheless, when innocent children are attacked and bullied because other children have a bigger arena to draw an audience, we are not protecting them enough. Parents need to be involved in their kids' lives and not just be Facebook friends with them.

Social media seems like a great way for a people to communicate with each other and it is. However, let's not make it out to be more than that because *it has not proven to be more than that*. There is no proof of concept for social media and social change. In some ways you could point to just as many problems it causes and think it is too much of a cost for the benefit it provides. We are not going to get rid of it, but there are ways we can improve the way we use it. We must either actually use social media to empower actual reform, or we are going to have to stop over glorifying what can be said in under 140 characters.

---

[6] "Cyber Bullying Statistics" http://www.bullyingstatistics.org/content/cyber-bullying-statistics.html, date accessed: 10 May 2013

Chapter 3:
They Don't Speak for All of Us

Even with the triumphs Generation Y can celebrate, there are as many, if not more shameful acts that leave questions in people's minds about the future where we will one day become leaders. In no way can we suggest that a few people speak for a generation. I myself cannot even speak for a generation. It is also not entirely known if all the men (if they should be called that) that I will describe below are the actual people to blame for the crimes they have allegedly committed since there are trials and investigations still occurring as this is written. That is not the entire issue of their addition to this chapter. They will be judged by our legal system, but the judgment should not extend beyond the individuals who have committed these crimes to be ascribed to a generation. I am not even saying that this has been a factor in the news's reporting on these cases. I bring up these recent events because they all have a common thread that is not only disturbing, but also something that should be addressed: they come from Generation Y.

James Holmes (25), Adam Lanza (20), Dzhokhar "Jahar" Tsarnaev (19), Tamerlan Tsarnaev (26), and now John Zawahri (23) have been accused of committing the latest acts of brutality on people of this country in 2012 and 2013. James Holmes is the current suspect in the case that involved 12 people being killed and 58 injured in a movie theatre in Aurora, Colorado. Adam Lanza was the man who allegedly shot twenty children and six adults at an elementary school in Newtown Connecticut. The Tsarnaev brothers are currently the suspects who are accused of detonating explosives in Boston,

Massachusetts, resulting in the killing of three people and injuring 264. John Zawahri is the latest story hitting headlines after he allegedly killed five people in Santa Monica, including his brother and father. I could not even get this book printed without another mass killing happening in this country. In between the time the Tsarnaev brothers were accused of the Boston Bombings and the events that happened in Santa Monica I tried releasing this book, but with the latest incidents involving a young person going on a shooting spree, it warranted an addition here.

Holmes, Lanza and Zawahri were three men allegedly acting on their own behalf with no inspired help. In the case involving the Tsarnaev brothers, the story is still developing at the time of this book's publication, but it is still clear that these men were self-radicalized by the youngest brother's own admission in early interrogations. Dzhokhar Tsarnaev claims not to have been involved with any known terrorist groups. These were four young adults on their own missions to reek havoc on innocent people, and as many as they could at once.

I call them "adults" because it does a great deal of disservice to call them "children" and "kids," as is frequently done on various news channels. They killed children and it is a fact that should be repeated that they were not kids themselves. Anyone who can muster up enough courage to grab a gun and kill another human being is no child. The country was outraged by their acts and rightfully so. Along with the outrage come anger, sadness and devastation for all those that are affected. Although we do everything we can to try to move on to still lead our lives, we cannot forget these emotions when travesties like this occur.

From these atrocious acts, much conversation sparked about gun control, mental health, and even immigration. However, in all of these instances, the issues sparked a lot of controversy and debate, only to lead to no action whatsoever. After the shootings in Newtown and Aurora, Americans were astonished with the amount of guns people have access to and the ease by which we can all acquire them. Regardless of all the hoopla and immediate outrage that people had, it quickly wore off and people were back to their normal lives. In fact, gun sales went up tremendously following these attacks because people feared the government would take their guns.

This generation is blamed for being the "Me Me Me Generation" as the Time has recently just declared us, but there could not be a more selfish people in this country who take a tragedy and turn it into a political problem, saying that they are the victims of a government trying to take away their guns. How could it be that the conversation regarding the death of innocent children get so convoluted that we are willing to protect our own rights to shoot another living thing over preventing another innocent being from dying as a result of a bullet? Our generation is entitled? How could it be that people feel they have a right to own something that is built to kill and are willing to fight for that right, but not fight for ways to prevent the future killers and mass murderers of this country from doing harm to another human being? Apparently the apple does not fall to far from the tree when it comes to "stupidity" because the narcissism that a group of people must have in protecting their own rights, while not caring about how this should never happen again is worse than our generation wanting to take a "selfie" (a picture of yourself). And then to say that you actually did think about the victims by claiming their should be more guns in schools, and everyone should be equipped with a gun for protection is completely ridiculous. This was merely the first and only suggestion to pacify an egotistical and entitled viewpoint of America that instead of ensuring more people are not shot, we put more guns into people's hands. Do you really think this is going to equate to less killings?

Let's say a fight breaks out in a dark and crowded room. One person has a gun. This person starts shooting. Much to his surprise, everyone in the room pulls out a gun and starts firing. Now there are hundreds of bullets flying in all directions because everyone has a gun to "protect" himself or herself. Is this a scenario that you want to be part of? Can you imagine a room full of inept and untrained gun owners trying to hit a single target? Okay, now let's consider what the "entitled" always say and play out the same scenario with one gunman. Let's say a fight starts out in the same dark and crowded place, but this time it is only one person with a gun. Before we go any further in this scenario, I would like to debunk any credibility to this and not give it any value because the real solution is that no one should have that gun to begin with. Why is this not a possibility? I will tell you. It is because the minute someone posits that as an idea, they are called un-American. What we end up doing is settling for absolutely no change whatsoever because the narcissistic groups that value their own right to a gun over a stranger's life throw around ridiculous accusations against people for trying keep this country safer.

The only legislation that was even close to passing was a bill that required laughable background searches for people buying guns, but essentially included a "friends and family plan" that undermined the entire premise. The reason why this bill was completely baseless is because a gun sale could be made without a background check, as long as the buyer was a friend. I could just see the conversations now.

"Nice to meet you," says the gun seller.

"You too. What is your name?" asks the gun buyer.

"My name is Huck. And you?" replies the seller.

"I am Chuck. We have been friends for the past two minutes, how about you sell me a semi-automatic?"

"That sounds great. Have a round of ammunition on me. We have been friends long enough that I trust you, pal."

Despite 90% of Americans wanting background checks for people trying to buy guns, even this watered down bill still did not pass.

Regardless of your party affiliation, the question remains: how can 90% of a people want something and it not become the law of the land? The answer lies in the very heart of the way people think today. In today's world of "I want it now," our visceral reactions demand an equally quick solution. This is not a Generation Y thing. This is a people thing. If something is not fixed in the immediate moments following an event, we eventually give up or move on to the next issue. What eventually won out as a result of the tragedies that struck us all are the longstanding ties that our lawmakers have with lobbyists and special interest groups. We allow these people to hold our country hostage from making comprehensible change that will satisfy the needs of a people who have certain rights without arming those who seek to do harm to us and take away the rights and lives of their victims.

The five young men who allegedly committed these heinous crimes were vigilantes of their own causes. They were not acting out of what any specific group thought was right or what someone told them they should do. They had no manifesto or guidelines to use with a specific end goal in mind. They targeted no one person in particular and had no other mission other than mass killings. If we can be outraged by what they allegedly have done, why are we not collectively rallying together behind legitimate causes to fight in a civilized manner for what we believe in? Instead, we think only about ourselves and rush out to the gun store out of some fear that the government will actually come through on a promise. With people who are capable of mustering up enough crazy to attack innocent people, we must prove as a generation and a nation that these kinds of people do not speak on our behalf. It should not take mass acts of violence for us to come together. The justice system is not enough to just ensure that those people who committed these acts never do it again. Of course those incarcerated will never commit such a crime on such a grand scale because they will either be locked away for life or be put to death if convicted. We also need to make sure no one else ever does these kinds of acts again. Even if these young people that allegedly committed these awful crimes had no other motive than mass killings, the spectacle by which they have committed these actions has been grand enough to cripple our resistance to atrocities of such a large scale. If you think I am wrong, nothing was done about it. More guns were bought. People were outraged. Nevertheless, we have not established means from preventing these kinds of acts again.

Sadly, this was the case. This book was published on Amazon as an e-book and before I could get it printed, these events transpired in Santa Monica. As this is a very recent incident as I write this, the story is not fully developed. What is clear is that this person killed his brother and father, and set fire to the home they were in. He then high-jacked a car with a woman inside, forcing her to drive him to a Santa Monica community college. Witnesses claimed that he was looking for people to shoot, spraying cars with bullets. He had an estimated 1,300 rounds of ammunition with him. It is unclear what his motives were, but it is very clear that we must do something about this and unless we have ways to prevent this from happening, people who should not get their hands on guns will continue to do so.

A troubling part of this conversation that was not brought up, but I fear to raise here is their age. I hate to bring it up because we do not need more reason for people to look down on young people. However, with it being a common detail in all the cases, there is clearly a problem. The fact that these were five young people says something about the state of our generation and the civil unrest we have as a people unguided to make the right choices. This is not a watered down distortion of the events. It is not that these men were misguided in a way that a kid smoking pot is. These were (again, allegedly) young people who mauled down innocent children and that is not forgotten. With the severity of the situation we do not want to lump a troubled teenager who battles with an identity crisis into the same group as a mass murderer. There is something that sends these young people to an extreme that is almost unexplainable and certainly beyond my ability to give a prognosis. Nevertheless, as a citizen of this country and person who sympathizes with the victims of this tragedy, we cannot sit by and call them outliers hoping no other outliers will exist in the country. If we just put them in a special category labeled "too crazy to resolve" then we are doing ourselves an injustice.

Lack of leaders to channel the passion young people have has left young people to their own devices to choose one of three paths when it comes to issues that concern us. I am sure there are more, as I hope not to generalize too much, but I will focus on these. A twenty-something left to his or her own devices can become a supporting bystander for something, a fighter for social good, or a vigilante of an ill-fated cause. Should a young person need a leader to point them in the right direction? Of course they do. Normally these "leaders" are found in the home. I say normally because as troubling as it is, the mother of the two brothers is thought to be behind their actions. Although this has not fully been understood, as the case is still under investigation, it is clear enough that children are sometimes just a product of a bad home. So what is to be done? We say that children need leaders so they do not grow up to be crazy killers when they grow up. Then we also say that the parents are to blame, and it is often the parents that make them this way. Do we have background checks for parents to have children? This of course is a crazy idea and no one would support that. Are the young people responsible for their actions? Yes, they must be accountable when they commit awful crimes. So all we can really do is raise our own children right and hope for the best, right? This seems like putting a lot of hope in billions of people to not instill young people with the wrong morals. Since we have to treat every individual as his or her own distinct person, we almost have no other choice.

Young people are not so impressionable that they depend on the need of someone to hold their hand. However, they have to learn what is right and wrong from somewhere. In no way am I going to play Freud and psychoanalyze the troubled minds of these men who may have not been loved enough as young children. It is also worth mentioning that a minority of people doing harm to others is not enough to suggest all young people need to be sat down and have a firm talking to. That being said there is nothing wrong with talking to children every once in a while to see if what their thoughts and opinions are on issues as this. It is traumatizing to have to witness and hear news about events like these. I also do not have kids so I would never tell people how to raise their children. Having been a child myself though, I know that even as a young kid I did have opinions. I was not as naïve as people thought I was and neither are your children. You would be surprised what your kids are talking about on the playground and if you don't know then maybe this is the conversation you should have with them at the dinner table. If we do not teach young people that these kinds of acts are not justified by making it a priority to enact some kind of change after a tragedy, then we are only left to brace for the next event.

Of course children know it is wrong to commit crimes. Of course they know that these are awful and horrible people who deserve to be punished to the fullest extent of the law, if they were the ones who committed the crimes. But that is the last part we need to focus on beyond these men. The law. It is either that the punishments are not foreboding enough to prevent these crimes or the motivation surpasses any threat of punishment. Why else would someone be willing to commit suicide in support of a cause?

The issue here is not with their age alone, but with the fact that they were able to conger up enough hatred in a short span of 19 years that would result in the killing of children, parents, cops, and humans like them. These kinds of acts are not justified at any age, but if societies have people in it as young as 25 who are willing to cause such massive destruction by shooting up a movie theatre, or a 19-year-old who is willing to detonate bombs to kill hundreds of people and we cannot find a solution to circumvent such acts from happening again, we are sending young people the wrong message. Forget not talking to them at the dinner table. If we fail to make it known to the parents and old people of this country that the government will not stand for these kinds of acts by doing something, anything about it then we might want to sit down our government officials at the dinner table and have a talk with them.

Instead of masses of young people fighting together for the improvement of our country with their voices and picket signs, we have a few people who fight their own self-motivated battles with guns and bombs. I am not going to presume it is because of a lack of face-to-face interaction that this generation is often blamed for with social media, but there is something wrong when it is easier to pick up a gun than it is to talk to someone.

Now there is a whole other issue about the sanity of people like these and whether or not they are mentally challenged. Holmes has entered a plea of not guilty by reason of insanity and Zawahri is thought to have faced mental issues. Fixing mental health problems in this country is not a distraction from the gun discussion that this country needs to have, again apparently. Both conversations need to be had. If Congress cannot handle two issues at the same time then young people are not the ones that have a problem with multitasking. Mental disorders in this country are overwhelmingly prevalent, as 26.2 percent of Americans over the age of 18 are diagnosed with some kind of disorder.[7] These are the known cases, so who knows how many are undiagnosed. More shocking is that in 2006 it was noted that 33,000 people committed suicide and 90% of those people had a mental disorder. I hate to group people who commit vicious crimes together with those who do not and say it takes a tragedy for people to want to do something about mental health, but we did not want even start talk about fixing the problems regarding mental health until one person decided to shoot up a school. Even still, we have done nothing. There are young people all over this country everyday battling with problems that they are not getting help for and it is not because this generation is just overly sensitive. Yet still, regardless of what motivates people to want to make actual changes, nothing has happened. The fact that travesty after travesty occurs and still nothing is done about mental health issues in this country does not make sense. Getting the help people need is our responsibility as a nation.

---

[7] NIMH, "The Numbers Count: Mental Disorders in America," *NIMH*, http://www.nimh.nih.gov/health/publications/the-numbers-count-mental-disorders-in-america/index.shtml, date accessed: 9 May 2013

Writing this section of the book, I can honestly tell you that I was hoping that by time I finished this entire project, there would be some major change that happened regarding gun control or at least we would revisit the debate. I even purposely did not finish this section until I was completely done, as news was constantly developing around the issues. I knew there would be developments, but I never imagined that we would not have solutions. Clearly the conversations regarding guns and mental health have stopped, and many people have moved on. Of course there are still those who valiantly fight for the victims and who want to see justice served. We will undoubtedly punish those who committed the vicious crimes described above, but we have done nothing to prevent it from happening again. It is both sickening and saddening that we cannot come together long enough to actually see action through. The fathers who stay up at night crying because their children will never graduate from elementary school, the wives who will only have pictures as tangible memories of their husbands who died, the older brothers who will not have a younger sibling to protect, the younger sister who now looks up to her younger sibling in heaven, the broken families and the tearful friends – who will answer to them? Who will reassure them that this will not happen again? Who will reassure *you* that this will not happen again? If we cannot look them in the eyes and tell them that we are done with the issues of gun violence, then why have we stopped talking about it?

Chapter 4:
They Don't Even Speak For Themselves

If the mainstream media is not going to allow intelligent and politically engaged young people to speak for themselves, who is going to be given the podium - whatever controls the ratings of course. Of course a young person shooting up a school will get headline news, but a young person with an opinion is never really broadcasted. A young person "shotgunning" a beer (drinking a beer really fast) will be the talk of the schoolyard, but we will not encourage young people to talk about politics. How else can you explain multiple seasons of Jersey Shore? Mainstream media and famous young people's managers have forced the wrong young people in front of America and turned the cameras on. We have somehow come to glorify teenage pregnancy, underage drinking, drug use and antics that do not accurately represent the youth of this nation. In no way shape or form am I going to compare the celebrity youth of this country to the rest, and I am not saying they are mass shooters or anything, but they are placed in a position to speak for us like no one else is. We live in a culture where the cast of Jersey Shore, Justin Bieber, and Honey Boo Boo dominate pop culture. Everyone complains that our generation is not intelligent, and the ones who get blamed for this the most are those that get paraded on television screens. The cast of Jersey Shore catches a lot of flack for what is edited together and called a television show, although with what goes on in that show, I am sure they would be happy if that is all they catch. I am not going to defend the actions of Bieber or Honey Boo Boo Child, but are we looking at the full picture?

Where are the parents when it comes to these child celebrities? Okay maybe this is not the best way to start, as many of these famous kids' parents are just as crazy. The Lohan family is a perfect example here. I am not even going to start in on Honey Boo Boo's mother June Boo Boo, and the other pageant moms who are equally as guilty of what seems like child abuse, but it is oftentimes fame that corrupts the entire family and not just the child. A stable family and upbringing can go a long way because not all childhood celebrities became complete monsters. Justin Timberlake, Christina Aguilera, Ryan Gosling, Brad Pitt and many others started their careers very young and tend to stay out of the tabloids. However, this generation of young rich people are doing all they can to torpedo their own careers and the reputation of this generation.

This brings us to Justin Bieber. I am not going to solely attack Bieber because I fear the wrath of the Beliebers. What I will say is that the kid's (yes he is still a child at only 19 years old and, if not in age, he still acts like a child) – this kid's behavior in 2013 has been questionable at best. Underage drinking, smoking marijuana, allegedly spitting on a man and threatening to kill him, inappropriate Anne Frank comments, frequent run-ins with the paparazzi and the list goes on that would make people start to question his longevity as a performer, as well as his future prison record.

Bieber tried to set the record straight on his track record at a recent Billboards Music Award show when he was booed for receiving a Milestone award. In his acceptance speech, he targeted his doubters saying:

"I'm 19 years old. I think I'm doing a pretty good job. It should really be about the music. It should be about the craft that I'm making. This is not a gimmick. I'm an artist and I should be taken seriously. All this other bull should not be spoken of."[8]

There are a few problems with his statement and the first is his own admission. He is only 19 years old and he has already faced more flack than most celebrities will have their whole career. There is really no other person to blame for him putting himself in situations where he would be caught drinking or smoking weed. He is 19 so he should have enough sense to know that these kinds of actions are going to put him on the front page of TMZ and other tabloid magazines because everyone has a camera phone. It does not matter that he thinks he is "doing a pretty good job" because he lives in the public eye. *I* can think *I* am doing a pretty good job in *my* life because I am a nobody. Therefore my opinion is the only one that matters, aside from the people closest to me. However, he has millions of people "close" to him, watching his every move. When MSNBC or HBO picks me up for my own show, then this will be a different story (I thought inserting a winking face would be inappropriate here), but as of right now, Bieber has to answer for his actions to millions of people he calls fans, and even the millions more who do not like him. The "haters" will be equally as vigilant in hoping he fails, as those who want to see him succeed. The other problem

[8] Eurweb, "Justin Bieber Booed During Billboard Awards Speech," *Eurweb* http://www.eurweb.com/2013/05/justin-bieber-booed-during-billboard-speech-watch/, date accessed: 10 May 2013

with him being 19 is that his fan base is full of 12-year-old girls. Like it or not, there are people that look up to him and even though he should not be a role model to anyone, that will not stop someone from thinking that he is.

To his credit he is "taken seriously," but apparently not by the people he wants to take him seriously. Again, 12-year-old girls think he is an "artist." Everyone else that is not listening to his music only sees him as the obnoxious teenager who has gotten out of control. If he wants the "bull" to "not be spoken of" then he should not participate in the bull. And if he really wants to leave the fan base of 12-year-old girls behind, then man up and just say "bullshit." He is just in that awkward age that every other famous celebrity girl goes through when they do not want to do candy shop television shows or rainbow pop songs anymore and want to become adults. So instead of just doing more mature roles, they try to break their contracts with young audiences and pose naked or release a sex tape. Bieber is doing the same thing, but he has just turned to drugs, alcohol and alleged threats against people's lives. (All of the actions I say about him are of course "alleged" actions because I am sure he has lawyers as strong as his Belieber army.)

And because I fear his lawyers, and do not want to give him anymore space than he deserves, I will shift the gear a bit and put the spotlight on the people who are not taking enough blame. Bieber and whatever teenage drones they dig up are merely ways for a manager and a record company to make money. As long as he is in the press, they are appeased, despite the lack of a childhood he will have and the money he will need to spend on therapy when he grows older. The accomplices in

Bieber's downward spiral, and any other famous child star are the people writing their checks. In case you weren't sure, those aren't young people running the record companies and in charge of his finances. It is the old people in Bieber's camp who are there to supposedly "protect" him who are not telling him to stop what he is doing and think about his actions. Should anyone have to babysit a 19-year-old kid? No, but when they have a meeting about the next brand of cologne he is going to release, maybe they should review his behavior and talk about why he is hurting his own brand. Where is his manager or his publicist or the record label or the other people in control of his PR and his money? If he wants to be taken seriously, he should start with the people in control of his career and have a serious talk with him. Record companies are more than likely thinking that they have no stake in Bieber's personal life, but unfortunately they do. As a person and a cultural figure, they get the whole package. They do not just get the singer side of him because he is unfortunately more than that. He is a famous person, so they must manage every aspect of his life. The people who claim no responsibility for his actions are the ones who are allowing all of this to occur by not stopping it themselves because they could very easily control the situation. They pay him for crying out loud.

The reason why I put some blame on the older people for people like Bieber and the cast of Jersey Shore is because it all comes down to money. The Situation and Bieber are just puppets on strings controlled by the people who write their checks. Any publicity is good publicity, but it is great publicity for the people who own the record company or the television studio. They collect all the money without receiving any backlash. They find any unsuspecting child willing to sell his soul and sell out a generation to make a quick buck. If we want someone to blame for the way this generation is perceived, Bieber is not the only one to point the finger at. There is definitely need for him to take responsibility for his actions and not think that he is going to be given a free pass because he is famous. However, there is also need for some finger pointing in the direction of the people in charge who keep putting these kinds of young people in front of America and telling them that these are our representatives.

Try to imagine an upstanding young individual who was able to articulate himself or herself without a red cup in hand and a beer pong ball in the other. Could you ever imagine that kind of person on television or in front of large audiences trying to promote the success of this generation? That could never happen and Justin Bieber is not to blame for that. He does not own the record company. Snooki does not own MTV. Just like most other things on this planet, there are a few people who actually have the power to make decisions. Everyone else is just vying for enough attention to stay relevant.

Chapter 5:
Religiosity

This chapter will be short I can promise you. Religion is one of those subjects that must be addressed in a book like this, but it is also something I think this generation either accepts or it does not. Along with that, it is something I believe people should be more accepting of altogether – not necessarily religion, but the fact that some people believe in a particular faith, while others do not. Before I go any further, I am a Christian and I believe in God. I say this because despite my belief in religion, there are civil rights, political, scientific and other issues at stake that many people believe should not interfere with their belief systems. One group is not more entitled to life and liberty than another. One person's belief systems do not trump another, despite what many will want to believe. A person's religion does not get to become justification for mistreating, oppressing or denying rights to people who have a different belief system.

There is a growing trend that young people are turning away from religion and moving toward science. This is not simply because people have put so much more emphasis on science and technology in the media, in schools, in politics and what jobs are available, but that has a lot to do with it. Reports indicate that participation in the Catholic Church has decreased 5% and evangelical religions have noticed drops up to 10%.[9] There is also

---

[9] Andy Morgan, "Atheism Statistics Show Young People Losing Faith, But Data Does Not Tell Whole Story," PolicyMic,

more of a trend in which young people believe in some kind of higher power, but do not necessarily identify with one religion. I guess this is where I fit in to have full disclosure, but regardless of where any one person fits, young people are slowly turning away from the church and this is an undeniable fact.

I say there is not one reason for people turning away from churches because rarely is there ever one reason for anything. One thing that I often shine light on is social media. Believe me, I think it is a great tool, but it certainly something that is accountable for a change in culture in this country. As I stated before, social media and the Internet have allowed for the proliferation of information to be spread faster than ever before. Resultantly, people have more choices and can choose what they want to listen to and what they believe in. This does not stop with religion. Today, kids can read about any religion that exists and make a choice for themselves. Moreover, when older people try to use issues that young people care about with religion as the backdrop, it dilutes one argument to make the case for another. For instance, gay marriage is an important civil rights issue of this generation, but when religion becomes used to attack it, to young people, the rhetoric contradicts what many people think is the fundamental purpose of many religions: tolerance. We will talk about both of these issues in a little more detail, but we have to discuss the obvious elephant in the room and enter the science versus religion debate first.

---

http://www.policymic.com/articles/12140/atheism-statistics-show-young-people-losing-faith-but-data-does-not-tell-whole-story, date accessed 12 May 2013

Personally, I believe in science, evolution, global climate change and the advancement of technology. I can also believe that there is a being beyond our earth if I so choose. It's America after all. Instead of constantly pitting science against technology, we should not let personal beliefs get in the way of scientists, politicians and legislators trying to make the planet and world safer for everyone. Not everyone believes in the same God or adopts the same principles as everyone else. So the fact that we let religion dictate our political decisions means that we favor one religion over another.

Christianity, which brings along its own list of -isms, Atheism, Agnostics, Judaism, Islam, Buddhism, Hinduism, Unitarian Universalism, Wicca, Paganism, Druidry, and other religions make up this country. Forgive me atheists for putting you all in the list of religions, but when people try to "preach" about how God does not exist, it essentially becomes a religion of sorts. This is a different debate for a different book, but when you try to convince me that there is no God, what makes you any better than the people you criticize for trying to convince you that there isn't one? Everyone needs to go to his or her respective corners, live their own lives and let others live theirs. The point is I hear you. With all of these religions or anti-religions, there is no way we can or should make decisions based on religiosity. The only decision that should be made on religion is that people have a freedom to practice whatever they choose. Beyond that, religious beliefs do not belong in the political realm. They belong in your house. Just as marriage is something that anti-religious and religious people alike want to have the right to in their own homes despite whom they love. Abortions are a choice that the individual has to live with.

Contraception is definitely a choice that a couple must make for themselves. This kind of pillow talk should not leave people's bedrooms.

Now that we have covered the obvious, not in full detail of course, but let's talk about the role of the Internet and social media in religion. There are countless of other books that deal with the science/religion debate. Let's talk about something that is not often considered. Young people do not have to go to church anymore because sermons are available on YouTube. They do not have to buy the bible because they have access to whichever version they want on the Internet. They no longer have to abide by the religion of their grandmother because they can pick which religion they wish to follow by reading about it online. Before, the only religion you really heard about was the one that was practiced in your home. You either followed what your family practiced all of your life or eventually lost faith. Rarely would people switch religions. Now, young people have access to more options. They can see and experience different religions at early ages, learn more about them and identify with a belief system more in line with their own doctrines. This is not a bad thing (in my opinion of course). People should be able to follow the religion of their choice, or no religion at all if they want.

Personally it is not my interest to force someone else to follow the same religious belief system I have. It is a personal choice of mine to believe what I believe, which is why I will go no further on my beliefs. It is a personal choice to believe in God, heaven and religious morality. Nevertheless, living in this country we all agree to the same laws set forth by the government. What your god chooses to do with you beyond this planet is between you and your god. Everyone remembers the whole "separation of church and state" thing until it comes to issues that they care about. Then it is "their" rights infringe on the church. Forget about the other people who are denied rights. The whole infringement could be further from the goal of gay couples. All people are asking for is to be allowed the same rights as everyone else. This brings us to the next issue.

Using religion to say that gay men and women cannot get married, or that a woman cannot have an abortion, or that a couple cannot use contraception because it contradicts a religion's principles puts young people in a predicament where they are forced to choose. They have to either continue believing in their religion, or fight for what they believe is socially right. Not to mention the fact that the inflammatory rhetoric that often is accompanied with religious zealots attacking social issues in the name of some god gets people riled up and start to question the validity of the church.

It is not religion that is the issue here. Gun rights activists always like to say guns do not kill people because people kill people. It is not religion that is inherently bad to young people. It is the people who abuse it in order to make political statements and deny civil rights to other people. When "God Hates Fags" signs get used at rallies, protests and military funerals, people taint the principles of religion to satisfy their own bigotry.

Should we be alarmed that young people have turned away from their religious upbringings? No, not at all. Just because Generation Y has more options in terms of religious beliefs does not mean it is a generation of heathens. In fact it has the potential to lead to more tolerance and acceptance of different ideas and opinions – isn't that the aim of religion to begin with. As long as we all live honest and decent lives, who are we to judge the morals of others? All we can do is live our own lives and not try to force religion, or the lack of religion upon anyone.

Chapter 6:
Changing the World is My Occupation

There has been a culture shift in the way the young mind works. When I was a little younger, I used to hear about how young people wanted to change the world once they left college. I aspired to be in that similar place. I thought college would be a place where political action was rampant and creative minds were gathering to figure out how this world can be a better place to live. I graduated from Stanford University not too long ago and the main concern of most of the young people leaving school is what job they will get. No one wants to change the world anymore because everyone wants to be the next twenty-something billionaire like Mark Zuckerberg. Of course you can say that Zuckerberg changed the world, but we are talking about social change and not a change from MySpace to a user-friendlier interface, which still does not have a "Dislike" button by the way.

We reached a plateau on the amount of change we are willing to make, and the amount we are willing to take. In fact, some think we need to undo some of the changes and progress we have made to "restore" the country. Conservatives say all the time that they want to restore America back to the way it used to be, but I am not exactly sure what era they are talking about – the one where there was slavery for most of the 19th century, Japanese internment camps of the 1940s, severe xenophobia of the 1950s, brutal racism through the 1960s, the rampant rise of drugs in the 1970s, the restored xenophobia and declining economy of the 1980s, gender discrimination still ongoing, and all the other problems that are still unsolved in this country. It is hard to find a decade where it was good for everyone. The issue is not even about disrupting the status quo anymore. The problem we face is that people are satisfied with having just enough justice and are even willing to go backward. Sure a little bit of racism might ruin my day, but it is not keeping me from living my life, right? This is how we think. So the big question is should we be complaining? This is what our great- grandfathers and grandmothers fought for, right? They wanted us to have easier lives than they lived, right? They fought for us to get the BMW we drive to work everyday and the integrated schools we go to everyday. This is undeniably true and it is the job of every generation to make it better for the next one coming in. Just because we have it "good" though, does not mean everyone has it good or even "okay" for that matter.

People think of the issues we fight today as marginalized fights that only affect a few, or are beyond the borders of America's problems, so we should not address them. Immigration is an ongoing battle but because it does not affect the day to day of the average person it is not an issue we tackle head on. Gay marriage is a debate we have had for years, but because it is an issue behind closed doors, it is not at the forefront of the majority of people's minds. Because the effects of climate change will not change our daily lives, we do not care. That does not mean immigrants do not deserve our attention, or that gay men and women do not deserve equal rights, or that future generations do not deserve a green planet.

Instead, this generation has made its problem finding a job that will allow them to buy a Mercedes. Pop culture is such an easy target when we talk about this issue because it has been overstated that the glorification of fancy cars and jewelry propagated on television and mainstream media has made our children materialistic. Instead I want to put the feet to the fire of those who think they are helping this generation. Politicians and lawmakers look at the stats and become bean counters when it comes to the future of this country. For instance, they see we are failing in education, especially in subjects as science and math so the alarm bells go off and everyone rushes out the door hoping someone will put the fire out. What ends up happening is President Obama then goes on television and says that we, the young generation, should get jobs in math and science. We should all be computer programmers and work for Google. There is nothing wrong with these jobs, if that is what you want to do.

It is understandable that we should invest in the future of technology and we will need people to do that. We will need workers who love IT and who are interested in improving technology, but it is also true that there will always be more people more fascinated with using the tools instead of inventing them. That is why there is supply and demand. Not everyone is wired in a way that allows them to program a computer and we do a great deal of disservice to those who are making an impact in other fields by putting all the attention of this generation on a few industries. Nevertheless, the bean counters in Washington do not see it this way. For them it is a very rational thought process. In the best caveman text I can put here: Math, science – we fail. Math, science – we want win. Make kids math, science.

This country has a big problem in putting on its blinders and worrying about immediate issues. Yes, there are open jobs for computer programmers that pay well. As a result of that, this country has no problem telling kids that they should follow the job, instead of following what makes them happy or at least brings joy to their lives. Some kind of engineering degree in today's society is seen as the Holy Grail that will lead college graduates directly to the yellow brick road of riches and the Land of Oz. The Humanities have gotten such backlash recently that one would question the need to learn to read at all. This country used to be about teaching kids the three R's. Other than the clear fact that Arithmetic and Writing clearly do not start with an "R," this focus we once had in education has proved to be wrong by today's standards. Who should we blame? I know! The generations before ours did not properly prepare us for the future by adding science and technology into the forced alliteration. So, let's forget about the other stuff and tell kids they will only get a job even if they do not know how to write a sentence, just as long as they can write a line of code.

Now the hot topics have changed so that means a change in direction, right? Wrong. Instead of telling kids to go to college, we become overly specific and tell them they should get a degree in computer science while they are there. Then we tell them that a degree in anything else is useless because they cannot get a job. This has become our end game and the benchmark of success: can we get a job. There were once higher aspirations that this country had. Now of course I am showing my age here in my naïve optimism, but why shouldn't a generation be optimistic about the future of a country instead of wanting to settle?

What's worse than telling kids to only get a degree in computer science? Telling them to bypass college altogether and just get a computer science related job. Reading blogs and social media today you will find thousands of articles by college graduates making more money than they deserve telling people not to go to college. Of course there are thousands more telling students not to get a liberal arts degree, or a psychology degree or anything besides a computer science degree, but the biggest hypocrites are those who tell kids to bypass any form of higher education and just start working. What else can you amount to anyway? All we are good for are to become coders. What kind of justification could they possibly have in doing this? Some will go as far to say that college ready students should avoid college altogether because working will give them the experience they need in life to be successful. Mind you, these are people who have masters and doctorate degrees, simply trying to get viewers to their blog. College is not for everyone and this is very true. School is not for everyone. What is for everyone is a willingness to learn something. It might not be out of a textbook, but we all have passions that motivate us. If you can harness enough energy to put effort into what you really love and make a life out of that, you have gotten further in your life than most people ever will. College might be a step to getting there, and if you know that then it should be something that is valued. If schooling, training, or the military is going to give you the fulfillment you need in life, then this is what is best for you and the world. Changing the world is going to have to start from a place where we can thrive in our lives and provide for future generations. That means more than just settling for a job though.

You wonder why kids are no longer interested in politics and getting involved in social issues. It is because they are spending 20 hours a day in their rooms coding to build your websites for your political campaigns. We should not stop encouraging kids to enter these new fields, but we should definitely stop discouraging them from going into anything else. Telling kids to get a job instead of telling them to become great at something limits passion. This might all sound like fuzzy heartwarming stuff to many people, but think about the major complaints older people have of us. We are lazy, disinterested, not passionate, selfish, greedy, money hungry, materialistic, and unmotivated. I wonder why.

I cannot tell you how discouraging it was to graduate from college and run into a roadblock that I could possibly be unemployed. Doubt started to kick in and I thought the three years I worked to graduate were wasted. At the time I did not know there were two million other young people in the age group of 20-24 who were also unemployed, according to the Bureau of Labor Statistics.[10] If I had known this at the time, I just would have thought they were all just English majors like me not having a chance in this world to ever get a job. Everyone says that this tough job market is the reality that young people have to face and they should learn now how tough it is in the "real world" to get a job with anything short of an engineering degree. In personal experience, this could not be further from the truth. The reason I had such doubts is because all of the outside

---

[10] College Parents of America, "IS YOUR COLLEGE GRADUATE MOVING BACK HOME?," *College Parents of America,* http://www.collegeparents.org/members/resources/articles/your-college-graduate-moving-back-home, date accessed: 20 May 2013

voices started to settle in and I was convinced that I wasted a lot of time and work. Nevertheless, I found a job at a company where my work is valued and my opinions are accepted. I have met some of the most amazing people there and am very grateful for what I have. Not everyone has the same experiences after they leave college though.

There is tremendous pressure to enter the workforce. Not to mention that politicians, commencement day speakers, everyone on television tells us young people we need a job, but there is no place we hear it more than at home. Parents are ultimately out to protect us and keep us safe and they feel it is their responsibility to make sure we have a job to provide a life for ourselves. However, instead of parents today wanting kids to become doctors and lawyers like they used to, they want them to become computer programmers. They think these are the jobs that are going to protect us and keep us safe, when in reality, there is no "safe" when it comes to young people and the work force.

Age discrimination is a very real thing in this country, but it is not just for old people. With unemployment being the lowest for people between the ages of 20-24 at 13.2 percent than any other age group, it is clear that there is a problem with the workforce. Even in the age group of 25-34. The unemployment rate is 8.1 percent.[11] These numbers are devastating as a fifth of unemployed

---

[11] Elizabeth A. Freeman, "Discrimination Against Young Workers in the Workplace," *Chron,* http://smallbusiness.chron.com/discrimination-against-young-workers-workplace-46927.html, date accessed: 4 June 2013

people in this country are young people. For the lucky ones of us who are fortunate enough to be hired somewhere, the situation does not appear much better.

The reason why I say age discrimination applies to young people is because the laws that were put in place to "protect" older people are slap in the face of younger generations. The Age Discrimination in Employment Act (ADEA) became the law of the land in 1967. Understandably, this law tries to protect older people from being replaced by younger and cheaper labor. Why have a 40-year-old person work the job two twenty year olds will do for half the price? The law was put in place so that question could not be asked.

However, instead of me just giving what some would call a biased interpretation of the reasons this law went into effect, let me give you the Congressional Statement of Findings and Purpose:"

(a) The Congress hereby finds and declares that-

(1) in the face of rising productivity and affluence, older workers find themselves disadvantaged in their efforts to retain employment, and especially to regain employment when displaced from jobs;

(2) the setting of arbitrary age limits regardless of potential for job performance has become a common practice, and certain otherwise desirable practices may work to the disadvantage of older persons;

(3) the incidence of unemployment, especially long-term unemployment with

resultant deterioration of skill, morale, and employer acceptability is, relative to the younger ages, high among older workers; their numbers are great and growing; and their employment problems grave;

(4) the existence in industries affecting commerce, of arbitrary discrimination in employment because of age, burdens commerce and the free flow of goods in commerce.

(b) It is therefore the purpose of this chapter to promote employment of older persons based on their ability rather than age; to prohibit arbitrary age discrimination in employment; to help employers and workers find ways of meeting problems arising from the impact of age on employment.[12]

Before I go any further, I need to inform you that this law only applies to people over the age of 40. Doubt what I say? In section 631 of the law entitled "Age Limits" it states:

"The prohibitions in this chapter shall be limited to individuals who are at least 40 years of age."[13]

I know it sounds very contradicting that the law entitled

---

[12] U.S. Equal EmploymentOpportunity Commission, "The Age Discrimination in Employment Act of 1967," *U.S. Equal EmploymentOpportunity Commission* http://www.eeoc.gov/laws/statutes/adea.cfm, date accessed 4 June 2013

[13] ibid

"The Age Discrimination in Employment Act of 1967" would discriminate against workers under 40, but this is what it does. Lastly, before I go further, I must say that when the law was made it was justified. I also do not disagree with the entire law. Older people should not be fired before they can retire. Old people should not be discriminated because of their age, just as young people should not. Old people should not be replaced by other (younger) workers, simply because we are cheaper. That being said, I do not disagree with a law on discrimination of age, when it discriminates against age. Young people are left out of the workplace often enough, so a law preventing age discrimination should also include all ages. This law may have been justified at the time, but the justifications do not hold up today. This law assumes that somehow young people are already at an advantage, and in order to correct this "problem" older people must be given more opportunities to balance things out. Forget that it is always older people as managers. Forget it is always older people in charge of the younger people. Forget it is always older people making final decisions. Young people are the advantaged ones. This is evident in the very first reason why congress justifies this law. When it says, "older workers find themselves disadvantaged in their efforts to retain employment, and especially to regain employment when displaced from jobs" this might be true and was probably very true in 1967, but this does not apply solely to older people today. Young people make up the largest percent of unemployed people in this nation so it is actually hardest for them to find work, let alone a second job. Young people are also hired as interns and put other low-level entry jobs, and would never be placed in a job that was above their experience level. We are just out of college so of course our "morale" is going to be higher because we have not had our lives sucked out of us yet by working a job all our lives. (I am merely joking of course). Even still, our skills are untested and when we get a job, (if we get one) we are retrained anyway to the specifics of a given company. Older people may have deteriorating skills, but young people are often seen as too much hassle because we have to be taught new industries from the ground up so we do not get hired.

Age limits are ridiculous so I agree that this practice should be outlawed. That being said, that door opens both ways. Being passed up on a promotion or being overlooked because someone is young is equally ridiculous if the person is qualified. Equally so, it is ridiculous to say an entry-level job cannot be filled with an older person. These justifications end by saying that this chapter is "to promote employment of older persons based on their ability rather than age," and this could be the biggest safety net for older people, with nothing below young people to keep us safe. We are essentially on our own when it comes to the workforce until we become 40. Politicians, television personalities and our parents think they are helping us by telling us to get a job, but they are sending young people into the grinder where the odds are stacked against us.

It is actually the policy of many (most) companies to use "Last in, first out." It has even become so common that is given its acronym LIFO, and to that I say, "WTF?" How is it even close to acceptable to fire someone merely because they were the last one hired? That is exactly what the policy states. Make no mistake about this. This is merely to protect the older people with higher seniority and ousts the young kid who was just hired. No matter if the young person is more of an asset to the company than the older people or if they provide better ideas. None of the other circumstances matter because it is merely a numbers game. If you are young, clearly you must be replaceable so we will just find another know-nothing kid to fill the role when business picks up again. If you are old, you are "disadvantaged" because your skills are deteriorating and you do not have the motivation to do your job anymore. How can the government actually protect complacency and employees hiding in a company who are not doing anything productive? It is then acceptable to not have the same passion for a company when you get older because you are older. This sounds like a bunch of older people in congress making excuses for other older people like them.

This is where the whole entitlement thing becomes called into question. Young people are called entitled and narcissistic, but this law could easily be titled, "The Entitlement of Old Age in Employment Act." From the very first word of the law, it is just a list of excuses for why older people are deserving of more respect because they are old. Should a young person deserve respect at first handshake? Of course everyone should be given the same amount of respect. Respect is a human being thing, and not a pay scale thing. That is why there is a pay scale. Let's say there was blatant discrimination for young people in the workplace. Do you think it would be corrected? Of course not because this law prevents it from happening. It already assumes young people have too many advantages when it comes to work, so why give them more?

We are not going to turn this into the affirmative action debate on age, so I am not addressing the elephant in the room. It should be clear by now that absolute equality is the driving force behind this generation's motivations for a better country. That being said, it is unbelievable that a law banning the use of "age limits" would have a section labeled "Age Limits." It is also not enough to say, "well that's corporate America for you." This law tried to correct an issue that I am sure was relevant at the time. However, in today's day and age we, young people, as well as old people are the ones not being hired. We all are being looked at as not having the right skills, unless you can code. We, young and old, are not finding the jobs we need to support out lives and our families. Young people are not asking for more or better chances (as old people must have done in 1967 to deserve such a laughable law). We are asking for absolute equality where young and old people all have equal opportunities to find work.

Despite this, we live in this world – a world where young people are the selfish ones. We are the ones who ask for too much. All we ask for is what you tell us to get: a job. What happens now are old people send us into this work environment, a work environment that they have setup against us, and then tell us not to complain. Young people used to refuse this kind of treatment. They wanted to fight "The Man" and not *become* the man. They wanted to fight the system, and not just become another cog in the system. The only other answer young people have found to avoid the company politics is to own their own company. There are bazillions of startups all over this country where young people think their idea is going to revolutionize whatever industry they are entering. This is our generation's rebellion. Like I said, instead of fighting a corrupt system where young people are not the leaders in an organization, they have tried to create their own little companies to only become the inadequate managers they were trying to avoid.

No one is so naïve to the idea that people should live out in the streets and never think of their own personal wellbeing. However, it seems we have gone too far. We are willing to sacrifice relationships, the care of others, the compassion for this country and the planet because we want a high salary. I have had conversations with people and they say that the generation of world changers and the kids who wanted to make an impact has been tainted by the economy. The economy has put pressure on kids to get a job. College loans are keeping young people from following their dreams. Debt is keeping students from changing the world. That might all be true but it is exactly why young people should not stand for this kind of injustice. The debt that all of us are in right now is not our debt and we did not create it in this country. We did nothing to contribute to it, yet we are the ones who have to learn to code and be miserable (sorry CS majors) because some people in the government do not know how to balance a budget.

Sure it is a quick fix for a person not having to sit in front of a computer screen trying to figure out what the heck hadoop is to suggest that computer science is the only major worth pursuing, but if we are all willing to admit college is not for everyone, who sat in the room and got to decide that all college students should learn to code? There are many people who love coding and that is great for them. There are many more who get into coding because they feel they have no other choice to make a life for themselves. There are others who just do not subscribe to the idea that coding is the only skill to secure a happy future. Debt is not new. College loans are not new. All of these things have kept families up at night for years. The difference is the answer we have to such problems. The answers being given today just do not suffice.

This is a culture issue we have in which what we hope for out of our young people is a well paying job. If you can get a job that you love then you are ahead of the game. If you cannot, just remember that you are not alone and it is not because you majored in the wrong subject in college. Some people might claim that this generation's fascination with jobs on the economy. College loans leave students with a surmounting debt that they can almost never pay back. Graduating from high school leaves students with no other choice but to enter the workforce because families cannot afford to pay for college. If all of these things are the case, why are young people not outraged? "You only live once" (YOLO) is not just a saying, it is a truth. That being the case, if you are being robbed of opportunities in the one life you get to live then these kinds of injustices should not be left to other people to decide. Besides, if you really want to avoid useless politics, the workforce is the last place you want to enter – it is a Petri dish of politicking just to keep your job.

Chapter 7:
You're Ignoring Our Issues and We're Ignoring Yours

Sorry, but this book is going to get a bit more political as we go, but it is out of a matter of importance. The world in 2013 looks a lot different than it has ever looked. We face a whole new crop of problems that were never thought imaginable, not by the forefathers of this country, and not by people even fifty years ago. No one foresaw the invention of the atomic bomb or automatic machine guns when the constitution was drafted. No one knew there would be an Internet that would keep track of all of our personal records. Just as no one could see these things coming, we have no idea what technology has in store for us in the next fifty years. What we can do though is address the issues we have today in order to prevent the tragedies and atrocities this country has faced as a result of an ever-changing culture of people.

Race is a sensitive enough topic, so why not talk about it here? This shouldn't make anyone upset, but of course you probably did not sense my sarcasm. Racism in this country is not dead. Racism is not dead. Racism is not dead. I said it three times so that what comes next is not shocking. Racism is not dead (a fourth), but it is dying. Please understand that I hate nothing more than to boil things down to color. I do not like to say, "black people this" or "white people that," but for the sake of talking about the history of this country, I am left with no other choice. White males used to have a preponderance of power in this country. White people may still have a dominant role in fortune 500 companies and in other places of power, but the makeup of this country is changing and becoming diverse.

Many people like to say racism is over because of the progress we have made as a nation (putting aside those that remain secretly racist while touting racism is dead). President Obama was elected twice, so racism must be dead, right? We cannot have single acts of racial unity to wash away multiple acts of racial division. The glue that is President Obama's election and reelection is not enough to hold this country together forever, and it does a great disservice to allow true racists in this country to hide behind a shadow of a black person being elected president. What we can say is that with the election of President Obama, a man of mixed race like so many other people in this country, is that race is becoming a facet of people we consider much less than we ever have before. This is why I say racism is dying because many would have never expected to see a black president, but that does not mean racism is gone forever.

Institutionalized slavery is dead in the United States. This is probably a premise we can agree with for the most part when it comes to America. However, racism and slavery are two different things. Living in 2013, we are far removed from racism. I can only read about it in books, just like everyone else can. I will never know the actual experiences that others endured in order for me to live this life. Since the times of slavery, race has always been a topic of conversation in America. That is out of necessity, but in constantly bringing it up, this has also been its own enemy. In 2013, people have become desensitized to racism to the point that they do not even want to hear it said anymore, so they would rather say that it is over entirely than actually deal with it. That does not make it right by any means and we have to be careful when we say that racism is completely gone because doing that would be grossly inaccurate. Saying that it is not as bad as it was before is acknowledging the work of people who died to ensure that.

People in this country think it is a grave injustice to even say racism is dying, and this I cannot understand. People died to get us to where we are now in terms of civil rights progress. A war was fought over the states' rights to control many aspects of this country, one being slavery. Civil rights were fought to give people equal rights. If we do not think that there has been progress and that race is diminishing, our ancestors died in vane. People like me are acknowledging the work they did for civil rights by saying we live in a *less* racist country – not diluting what they did.

2013 looks nothing like 1830, 1930, 1940, '50, '60, '70, or even 1980. We do not live in our grandparents' generation where race is a factor in everyday life because black and white issues are much more colorful than ever before. Minorities are becoming the majority and this is not a source of achievement or accomplishment – it is just a fact. In order for people to understand how and why young people think less of racism than our grandparents, we are going to have to do a little math. Young babies are born and they just so happen to be minority babies. They will then become young children, grow up to teenagers and will then become young adults. This is pretty much the cycle of life. Even though that seemed very simple, it is apparently misunderstood by many older people who think racism is just as bad as it ever was. This cycle of life is just for one person. Now multiply that by a million, or even a billion. Millions of young "minorities" are being born in this country. To recap, minority babies become minority young adults, and these minority young adults are becoming the majority, meaning diversity is evermore prevalent than ever before – not racism. Many young people today are far less concerned with racism than they were ever before because they are the race that is usually the topic of being oppressed. But just to hammer home this numbers game idea - Unless people are becoming racist of their own kind, the idea of race is blurred so much that it is almost impossible to know what anyone is anymore. This also does not account for young white men and women who are simply not racists and also grow up surrounded by this kind of diversity. They do not consider race in their everyday lives either.

The other reason race is *less* of an issue by young people today is because racism is taught. No one is born a racist and it is not a genetic disposition to be born with hatred for another human being. We owe it to our parents and grandparents for fighting for rights of all people. We also owe it to them for not passing down hatred to us. Racism is deep emotion has to be learned from somewhere, so if racism is going to stop completely but no one wants to do anything about it, we are either going to have to stop listening to those who indoctrinate the young with lies and hatred, or just wait until these kinds of ideas all die out. If you don't believe in evolution, you might have a hard time with this next set of ideas but racist people really are a minority in this country. The less those ideas are given voice and the less young people stop giving credence to such bigotry and fight it head on, the more racism will die out in this country.

The problem in thinking that racism is the same monster that it used to be is that racism traditionally stemmed from a power position. White men and women had a disproportionate amount of power and therefore could oppress minorities. Hatred of an entire group had power associated with it because white men and women owned everything. Minorities could not own property, vote, and were not even considered humans. I know the whole debate about white women having less power than white men, but let's deal with one sensitive subject at a time. Why I say that racism was often thought to be about power is because it was common opinion that only white people could be racists. Now there is a whole idea about reverse racism in which white people are treated unfairly as a result of minorities getting "special treatment." First of all, there is no such thing as reverse racism. The term in and of itself is a little racist. Racism is racism and one race does not own it. Power is not completely balanced, but there is more equality than before. That being said, anything less than complete equality is not enough. Furthermore, if a black person derides a white person or mistreats them because they are white, then this is pure and flat out racism. If an Asian person says something negative towards, or discriminates against a Latino person, then this is racism. White Americans are not the only ones in this country that can be prejudiced. The more we try to victimize and find an enemy, the more this country pits one against another and that is the true evil of racism. In an ideal world, we could get to a place where race is not even a discussion. Does anyone talk about the size of your left big toe? This is a feature of one's body just as much as the color of one's skin is.

Of course there is a history of racial oppression that should not be forgotten, so this is why race is still discussed whereas people's left big toes are not. Our histories must never be forgotten, but we must stop trying to relive them. The injustices of the past should not be an excuse for having prejudiced ideas today. We use history as a lesson to guide us and teach us to not make the same mistakes. History is not a means to continue to hold a grudge for something you were not living to experience. The bitterness surely should be gone by now. The issue of race is much in line with gang mentality. This might be a jarring analogy to some, but bear with me. One gang member from gang A does something bad to a rival gang member in gang B. Gang B retaliates. This cycle of retaliation continues and revenge continues, and although the new members of the gang are fighting on behalf of people they never knew and are so far removed from, they fight anyway because the people before them did. Thinking that you deserve something because of the way your ancestors were treated is not why they died. If you an encounter a racist person today, it is not an entire race (or another rival gang) you now have a problem with. It is one individual racist that you have a problem with. The "other" race is not an enemy because one bad person did something to you. One person's bigotry does not represent an entire people. Our ancestors of every color died because they wanted to make this country a place where race would not be a constant hindrance to your life as it was for them. The issues of race that are viable today are the ones that *happen* today. Therefore, in our country we do not just have a black and white issue. We have a people issue.

There are more people in this nation than ever before and there are many different races and ethnicities people identify with than ever before. Immigration reform is the new civil rights in this country and we are going to have to address it; not only that, we should for the sake of the innocent people legally trying to enter this country and the children born here to parents who may have come here illegally. Being born on American soil makes you a citizen so the status of their parents is in the balance because we fail to act on issues concerning this country today.

We should want racism to diminish. It should just be understood that young people in this country want to move forward. We do not want racism to exist anymore like anyone else even if this is an impossible battle, as racism may exist forever in countries beyond the United States. We however acknowledge and are appreciative of those that died, our parents that suffered and the problems many have faced in order for us to hold ideas that people think are naïve. No one should feel betrayed that racism is not the same problem it was in the 1960s. That is what you protested for, so be proud of the work that was done and stay just as passionate about the work that can still be done. There are still battles to win, but because of our ancestors' fights we can live in a country where it is not a fight that we must have everyday just to live a normal life.

In the ideal world it would be nice to say that no one will ever judge another because of the color of one's skin. I would hate to be so skeptical to think that racism is so embedded in our history that it will forever plague our futures. That being said, I have hope that the majority will prevail in this instance. I also hope that racism is not just replaced with some other superficial feature of our lives like money.

Economics is what many consider to be the race situation of the twenty-first century. It is not visible on one's skin, but it does create division between us. The other big difference in this case is the minority is the one with all the power. Remember that whole one percent and ninety-nine percent debacle that lasted only as long as every other fleeting movement in this century? Well despite the lack of cohesion and focus the Occupy Movement had, it was inspired for good reason. The top one percent in the U.S. earned approximately 93% of the nation's income growth in 2010.[14] The top one percent saw an increase of 5.5% wealth in 2011, while the bottom 80% of the country saw an earnings decrease of 1.7 percent. That's right, you read decrease. 96 million households in this country make up the 80 percent of the nation, which means is an ever-present problem in this country we are not addressing. In 2011, the gap between the rich and the poor has been the widest it's been in four decades. The idea of the American Dream is dead for this generation, as the rich only get richer and the poor are left with nothing but a dream.

The greatest ideal of this country was that a dream could one day be realized, but now people are mostly just trying to figure out how to get by. There used to be an "American Dream" in this country, but for this generation and many more people, that dream is just a nightmare that we cannot wake up from. The poverty line for a single person is $11,490. There are 45.8 million people in this country that are poor and below this line,

---

[14] Peter Robison, "Top 1% Got 93% of Income Growth as Rich-Poor Gap Widened," Bloomberg, http://www.bloomberg.com/news/2012-10-02/top-1-got-93-of-income-growth-as-rich-poor-gap-widened.html, date accessed 20 May 2013

which makes up about 15% of the population.[15] People cannot afford groceries let alone healthcare and when you look at the numbers, it is pretty telling of the state of our nation. There are 45.8 million poor people in this country and 45.7 million Americans do not have health insurance, and that is not counting the 16 million more who are under-insured with inadequate protection.

To put this into perspective, let us look at the numbers in a different context. The entire populations of Texas and New York combined do not reach 45.7 million people (45.5 million to be exact). Imagine the entire nation has healthcare, except for two of the United States' largest states. I know Texas likes to think of itself as its own nation, but when the population of two large states would go without being covered for their health issues, we need to reevaluate our position as having the greatest healthcare in the world. If Texas and New York were to leave the union, these two states would have to fend for themselves, hoping no citizen got sick or needed to go to a doctor for any reason so as not to come out of pocket for medical treatment. That is the reality. Just because all of the people are not populated in just two areas where they would be more visible, does not mean they are invisible.

Before anyone starts to think that the 16 million number of under-insured people is small, let's play this context game one more time. The country of Chile has

---

[15] Erin McClarri, "There may be millions more poor people," *NBC News,* http://inplainsight.nbcnews.com/ news/2013/05/03/176717 53-there-may-be-millions-more-poor-people-in-the-us-than-you-think?lite, date accessed 20 May 2013

approximately 16 million people living in it. Chile certainly has healthcare provided by their government, but could you imagine an entire country that size, with that many people not having adequate healthcare? 16 million people would have to find the best help with what they could afford, if anything at all. In the United States, that is the reality. There are 16 million people that do not have access to adequate doctors, physicians, or the help they need. By the numbers, the United States has an entire country within it that does not have access to proper health coverage. Just because people have some form of healthcare insurance does not mean they are insured from high bills, debt or even will receive care at all. Simply because the 16 million people are not clustered in one country does not mean they do not exist.

In this country, President Obama has tried what other presidents have failed to do – he has passed healthcare reform. It is his vision to see that everyone has healthcare, despite wavering on the idea to have universal healthcare. Even though we have settled on a compromise for healthcare reform that still does not go far enough, there are people who want to get rid of it altogether. In 2013, Obamacare has been brought to a vote so that Republicans can try to repeal it for the 37th time. After President Obama was elected the second time, the American people pretty much made their vote on this issue. We have a law of the land and now it is constantly called into question because we have a political system now that cares more about party affiliations than it does about the people. Why would our congress vote on something that has already proven not to work 36 times, well it really is quite simple.

Speaker of the House John Boehner wanted to give the

newly elected congress that got their new roles in 2012 a shot at taking down Obamacare. The newly elected congress members need a demonstrative show of faith that they are staying true to their base. The conservatives that elected the Republican and Tea Party congressman, although a minority in the entire country are not fans of the Obama healthcare plan set to go into effect on January 1, 2014. Coincidentally enough, the next round of elections for congress is in 2014. Conspiracy theorist? I think not. This is what Boehner has said in his justification for voting on something for a 37th time. Boehner said, "We've got 70 new members who have not had an opportunity to vote on the president's health care law. Frankly they've been asking for an opportunity to vote on it."[16] It goes without saying that the House is currently by Republicans and the Senate is run by Democrats. Because of that, the entire vote is an exercise in futility, as the liberals are not going to budge on this issue. They have already made that pretty clear 36 other times. The new 70 members just need to be able to go back to their base the next election season and have a proven record of disagreeing with the bill.

While over 45 million people hope and pray they never get sick because they literally cannot afford it, our congress is playing games with our lives to put on a façade that they are running our government. The illusion of doing work does not just happen in the cubicles at your office building. The entire country is run

---

[16] Tess VandenDolder, "37th Time's the Charm: House Votes to Repeal Obamacare, AGAIN," *In The Capital,* http://inthecapital.streetwise.co/2013/05/16/37th-times-the-charm-house-votes-to-repeal-obamacare-again/, 20 May 2013

by a circus without a ringleader. The lions are running wild, the two-headed "freaks" are scaring the children and the bearded lady has gotten loose again. I mean why is Sarah Palin still relevant? If you drew any conclusions based on that last statement, it is your own fault because I only placed the two sentences next to each other. I implied nothing.

This is not the first time our government has been compared to a circus, but is my lack of creativity in creating another analogy really the problem? The issue is we have this problem in our country where we simply do not seem to care about actual issues that are happening. Perhaps you can blame this on young people not yet being beaten by disappointment, but our lack of jadedness only makes us have expectations. Expectations when it comes to the government really are dangerous, unless your expectations are low. When young people look at a number like 45 million we see a gross injustice. When young people hear about a single act of racism we cringe. Politicians see it as a minority of the country that will never vote for them anyway so why bother. They see racism as a hot button issue that could prevent them from being elected. This nation is divided between the haves and have-nots – those that have hope for this country and those that do not. Young people do not have a monopoly on hope, but they expect more from a country that we constantly hear is the greatest nation in the world. It is time that we start acting like it again in which every person in the country is the greatest it can be.

The American Dream used to be having a house with a fence, a dog, and a few kids. Now this ideal has completely been changed, as people cannot afford to own a home, have children or feed a dog. The middle class is the driving force of the country, but the middle class has almost been crushed into non-existence. This is the country that young people are growing up in today. Work used to be something that a man or woman could take pride in. Having a job was almost a badge of honor and a symbol of being on your way to achieving that American Dream. Now a job is merely a way to support a family and keep food on the table. Children are growing up without their parents who have to work two jobs just to get by. Education is completely falling by the wayside, and in case old people were not sure, education is a very prevalent issue concerning young people today. There are so many problems this nation faces and yet we merely argue about a few things and cycle through them, never fixing anything as we go.

We get all worked up about an issue for a brief moment and then completely forget about it when the next wave of controversy hits. We are worse than the character from "Up" that keeps getting distracted by squirrels. This chapter started about race, but in the few pages since, a plethora of other concerns this country has left unanswered were brought up. I am not saying that race is irrelevant, but it is not our grandmother's country anymore. Some of the problems mentioned today are not even specific to this generation, as they were very relevant decades prior. You would think we would have solved them by now. That being said, instead of just being the whistleblower on these issues, what are we doing to improve them? If we want racial issues to improve, where has there been a legitimate Martin Luther King Jr. in the decades since his death? Instead of people complaining about injustice, stand up and fight for what is right. If we want the issues we face to stop plaguing our society we must own up to them and fix them. Conservatives complain all the time that they want a smaller government, but with that means the nation and more importantly, the people must be responsible for governing themselves. If the congress of disbanded elected officials cannot come together, I fear the power entrusted in an even more divided populace, who constantly focus on what separates us rather than what brings us together.

Squirrel!

Chapter 8:
Politicization without Representation

Everyone says that the younger generations need to take part in the political process. The youth should care about politics because they are the ones who are going to inherit the debt, the planet and the troubles created by those before them. If that is all true, and we are in fact doomed the way that everyone says we are unless we do something about it, then why are there no young people representing us in these political conversations? Turn on CNN, MSNBC, Headline News and Fox News and you will see much, much older people telling us how we should live our lives. If there is no one representing our viewpoints and our perspective in these conversations, then we are less inclined to become involved because we will always know that our opinions don't actually matter. We will be ushered out during election seasons to answer phones and be interns to get older people elected because they don't know how to use a Twitter, but then quickly pushed aside once the election is over.

Even the comedians are all old when it comes to politics. Turn on NBC, HBO, CBS, Comedy Central, etc. and you will find more grey hair than you will on a Hair Club for Men commercial. The Late Night talk show wars are all over appealing to the younger demographics but the youngest kid on the block is Jimmy Fallon at 39. From Stephen Colbert (49) to Jon Stewart (51) to Bill Maher (57), the political comedians are not getting any younger. These are all very funny and respected comics, but the fact that there is not a single person younger than 40, let alone under 30 whom young people see on television as one of their own, is absurd.

Rachel Maddow (40), Anderson Cooper (45), Greg Gutfeld (48), Bill O'Reilly (63), Wolf Blitzer (65), and the rest of the bunch that we get our political news from everyday are all over 40. People wonder why young Americans are not more involved in politics, but there is no one that looks like us, talking to us on a daily basis. (If any networks are looking I am available). Instead, we have the cast of Jersey Shore speaking for our generation, and as much as older people complain about the antics of people like "The Situation," it is the older people who keep green lighting these shows. If MTV, BET, VH1 or any of the other "young networks" want to be responsible for the way this generation is represented, then they should put on responsible programming.

There is no young person on mainstream media that is given the opportunity to reach out to fellow young people. What we do have is a bunch of older people trying to relate to us on some very superficial levels. Just having social media channels running along the bottom of the screen or at the end of a show does not mean you are connecting to young potential viewers. We can speak on behalf of ourselves; so telling us to get involved in politics does not mean just having enough passion every four years to collect enough energy to get us to a voting booth. Clearly there are issues this country faces other than electing a president. In the 2008 election, young people made up 18% of the voters, according to exit polls, and 19% in 2012.[17] From this, Obama won 66% of

---

[17] Pew Research, "Young Voters Supported Obama Less, But May Have Mattered More," *PewResearch Center for the People & the Press,* http://www.people-press.org/2012/11/26/young-voters-supported-obama-less-

young voters (ages 18-29) in 2008 over McCain and he won 60% of the young vote in 2012 over Romney.[18]

People tout all the time that young people played a crucial role in electing and reelecting President Obama. The numbers prove it. Obama has even supported many issues that young people care about, but that does not mean throwing us a bone every now and then warrants little to no representation in the political process after election seasons. This is by no means the fault of the government, although democracy is supposed to be a government run by the will of the people. This is more of a social acceptance issue that young people's opinions are not heard.

Although the statistics of young voters may have been promising for President Obama, they are not promising for the future of this country. Only 50% of young people between the ages of 18-29 were registered to vote in the 2013 election. Before anyone starts bragging about the 50% of young people engaged enough to get off their couch, this is the lowest percentage of young people registering to vote since 1999.[19] For all other age demographics, at least 70% of people are registered. The political process has proven it is broken time an time again as of late, but could it be that young people saw the writing on the wall a little sooner and disengaged? Did

---

but-may-have-mattered-more/, date accessed 15 May 2013

[18] ibid

[19] Pew Research, "Youth Engagement Falls; Registration Also Declines," *PewResearch Center for the People & the Press, http://www.people-press.org/2012/09/28/youth-engagement-falls-registration-also-declines/, date accessed 16 May 2013*

young people give up on the political process because they know that a do-nothing congress dominates our country?

President Obama gave a commencement speech in 2013 to the Ohio State University graduating class and he spoke to the problem of disinterest and distrust with the government. He claimed

> "You've grown up hearing voices that incessantly warn of government as nothing more than some separate, sinister entity that's at the root of all our problems. You should reject these voices. Because what these suggest is that somehow our brave, creative, unique experiment in self-rule is just a sham with which we can't be trusted."[20]

He later went on to pose a challenge to the future of our nation, "I dare you, Class of 2013, to do better. I dare you to dream bigger." As a young person and as a person daring to dream myself, I would posit the same challenge and gesture toward the people who are supposed to be representing our best interests. It is not the job of citizens to blindly follow any one political party, but to be critical of our current state of affairs and make politicians do their jobs, as they expect us to do. So it is not just about the Class of 2013 doing "better," but it is also the job of our government officials to make sure the system works, despite the fact that they possibly have a worse

---

[20] Caroline Bankoff, "President Obama Begs Class of 2013 Not to Give Up on the Government," NY Mag, http://nymag.com/daily/intelligencer/2013/05/obama-tells-graduates-to-make-better-government.html, date accessed 21 May 2013

reputation than Generation Y. If the government is viewed as a "separate, sinister entity" then there is a failing that is rooted in the people we elect, not just with the people who elect them.

Do you want to know why young people do not get involved in the political process? The political process is full of lies, deceit and everyday controversy. To put it simply: there is too much politics in politics. High school isn't even as bad as the dealings in Washington D.C. Take the current "scandals" rocking the U.S. today that could leave a unfavorable impression on Obama's administration. These quasi-scandals mostly look bad at first glance, or if you are watching FOX News then they are signs of Obama's evilness. The scandals I am talking about are of course IRS-gate, AP-gate, and Benghazi-gate. Let's start with the I.R.S. scandal. (I do not want any unwarranted delving into my taxes so I am going to be careful in my wording here.)

The IRS is reported to have unfairly targeted conservative groups demanding details about the groups' members and activities. The IRS singled out groups with words like "Tea Party" and "patriot" in their titles, to what the IRS officials are claiming to be the result of poor management. Clearly this is a textbook definition of overreaching, but it is also worth noting that it was not Obama's hands in the pockets of these conservative groups. The Obama administration does not need to run from the scene of the crime because they weren't there to begin with. The head of the agency Steven Miller said, "I did not mislead Congress or the American people. I think what happened here is that foolish mistakes were made by people trying to be more efficient."[21] First of all there is a lot wrong with what he said. The first is that at no time ever is the IRS or anything that they do "efficient." (Anyone at the IRS should understand that as a joke). The second is what he was really trying to say without saying it is that if there were any people of this country looking to scam the American people, it would be Tea Party activists. Why else would they feel like they were being "efficient" by targeting groups with "Tea Party" in their name? Well let's see – the whole basis of the Tea Party is that they do not believe in taxes. The I.R.S deals with taxes. It all seems to add up. I am not saying the Tea Party is full of scam artists (the IRS did). I am just saying that perceptions exist for a reason. We can get to this in a later chapter, but let's stay on the scandal.

Immediately following the story hitting the news, The Obama administration fell under attack. Obama himself had to come out and say that the acts were deplorable and unacceptable. He then went on to ensure that Miller resigned. Nonetheless, in a world where we can now say something and not have any truth support it, or even take ownership that we said it, the fault has somehow stayed with Obama. It is always amazing to me that when something cannot be directly blamed on President Obama himself, it is always the fault of the Obama administration. As long as they can say "Obama," everyone seems satisfied. The buck stops with him, as many people like to say. Since the truth is often hard to find in piles of lies, I will try to make sense of this and

---

[21] Chicago Tribune, "IRS scandal: Lawmakers accuse IRS officials of lying," *Chicago Tribune,* http://www.chicagotribune.com/news/chi-irs-scandal-20130517,0,3819213.story, date accessed 22 May 2013

deliver some facts.

The truth is the IRS is a bureau of the Treasury Department, which is an executive agency within the federal government. It is the president that nominates the head or chief executive of the IRS. Now before conservatives stop reading and say "Gotcha Obama!" and think that President Obama conspired to target conservative groups during the election, everyone should also know that former President Bush was the one who elected the man in charge and the Senate confirmed the nomination. Now here is the real deal breaker you are not going to hear from conspiracy theorists. The law prohibits the president, vice president and any members of the executive office from directly or indirectly requesting any officer of the IRS to conduct or terminate an audit of any taxpayer in the United States.

The administration is bound by law to *not get involved* in the process of, or the dealings of the IRS, other than to hire and fire the person in charge. This is the law. Before the coffin is closed on this one, when Republicans questioned Miller on whether or not President Obama knew about this targeting, Miller responded that this "would be a violation of law."[22] Any officials that knew in the administration would have been breaking the law if they told the president. Thus, to keep him from violating any laws and actually become impeachable, President Obama was not told. Before anyone makes

---

[22] Jonathan Weisman, "Republicans Expand I.R.S. Inquiry, With Eye on White House," *NY times,* http://www.nytimes.com/2013/05/18/us/politics/irs-scandal-congressional-hearings.html?_r=0, date accessed 21 May 2013

another Nixon comparison or tries to suggest that the Obama administration would not break the law, neither President Obama, nor his administration has walked away from this ordeal and are cooperating fully. Everyone is quick to say that this is a cover-up, but who only covers up a scandal for a mere few days and then openly discusses the issues?

This brings us to the Benghazi attack.

On the anniversary of September 11, in 2012 an attack was made at Benghazi in Libya. The attack was against the consulate building and a nearby CIA annex that resulted in the death of four Americans, Tyrone S. Woods, Glen Doherty, Sean Smith and J. Christopher Stevens. At first, it was thought and reported that the attack was prompted by a video released on YouTube, but the U.S. State Department investigated and found out that it was a premeditated attack by Islamist extremists. Over 100 gunmen attacked the consulate at 9:40 PM and immediately phone calls were made to the embassy in Tripoli, Washington, a Libyan brigade, and a U.S. quick reaction force located approximately a mile away. On a third phone call attempt, Ambassador Stevens was able to reach the Deputy Chief of Mission Gregory Hicks to inform him of the attack. The Benghazi CIA annex was also called, so the CIA's Global Response Staff, including security operative Tyrone S. Woods, decided to try and rescue the victims. Upon arriving at the scene, the rescuers were able to secure some survivors, but had not found Stevens. While transporting the victims, the vehicle was hit with gunfire, but it was able to return to its final destination. It was later found out that Ambassador Stevens had died. The four bodies were then returned back to the U.S.

After the attack, it was released that a YouTube video was the reason for the attack and that there were protests prior, but it was later understood that there were no protests, and the attack was preplanned. It had nothing to do with the YouTube video. Although these are now the facts, these are also the facts that the Obama administration fully admits to. During and immediately after the attack, it was said by many people from the president's camp that the case was developing. President Obama had actually called the attack an "act of terror" the next day on September 12, 2012. He later used the same phrase the day after that in Vegas. Now there is uproar because he did not use the phrase "act of terrorism."[23] It is this kind of hairsplitting that derails the political process and keeps people from being actually interested in having productive debates. It does not matter that he did not add an –ism at the end of his sentence. This does not warrant the witch-hunt media has embarked on in hopes a "Deep Throat" will surface to expose President Obama's secret dealings with terrorists. We get too distracted by trivialities that people start to see through the lies and eventually disengage from the noise.

It is also amazing that in the weeks that the blame for the attacks turn to Hilary Clinton for her involvement in the Benghazi debacle as Secretary of State, that everyone

---

[23] Glenn Kessler, "Obama's claim he called Benghazi an 'act of terrorism,'" *The Washington Post*, http://www.washingtonpost.com/blogs/fact-checker/post/obamas-claim-he-called-benghazi-an-act-of-terrorism/2013/05/13/7b65b83e-bc14-11e2-97d4-a479289a31f9_blog.html, date accessed 20 May 2013

starts talking about the 2016 election. The dissenters have already given up hope that the Benghazi attack can be blamed on the president, so they found a new person to point the blame at. As early as 2013, pundits are already claiming how the Benghazi attack is hurting the chances of a woman who has not even said she plans on running for president yet. If it is the hopes of Republicans that they can cut her at the heels and taint the Obama Administration in the process then this is why young people are tired of politics. If President Obama actually did conspire to have the IRS target conservative groups, and purposely did not help the consulate in Benghazi and aiding terrorists, and targeted the Associated Press for any other reason that to stop a terrorist attack, then this is also why young people are fed up with politics. We are so interested in demonizing each other, assigning blame for political agendas, and playing the "gotcha" game that we waste more time chasing down conspiracies than we do actually solving the problems. We are currently playing the cooked spaghetti game, throwing everything against the wall, hoping one of them is good enough to stick.

The problem with this strategy is all of these stories are more media hype than actually legitimate cover-ups. It is only so long before people's minds are filled with mass proliferation of lies that they either start to believe them, or do not know what to believe. In either case, this creates a firm distrust in the government that cannot be erased. The Obama administration will forever be plagued with these scandals, regardless of the legitimacy to any of them.

To give you a personal example as an anecdote, I saw a meme on a website. (To put it simply, a meme is basically what young people call funny pictures.) In this meme, there was a flat out lie that suggested Obama should be impeached like Nixon was impeached for covering up crimes. There are a few problems. Nixon was never impeached. He resigned before any formal act was made against him. Secondly, there was an actual cover-up when it came to Nixon. The Obama administration reported the facts they had at the time and then when the case developed, reported the facts they had learned as time went on.

When someone on the website posted the picture to his or her wall it did not take long before a fact checker will enter the conversation. After reminding the original poster that Nixon was never impeached, there was no apology or retraction for making false comparisons. In fact, the original poster tried to defend the idea that President Obama was still worse than Nixon. This might seem like a very minor and personal matter between strangers, but if this is happening all over the world, then we will never have truths in this country. It is completely okay to spread lies, hoping that people know what information to decipher as truth and what should be seen as lies.

Information, regardless if it is truth or lies is spread as fast as you can click and this is the problem I am speaking of when I talk about the rapidity of social media. I hate to harp on it, but it is the culprit in many of our social problems. People complain about transparency, but when the president finds out information at the same time as the American people, we are getting information too fast. It is also then impossible to be forthcoming because we all know before his speechwriters can figure out how to spin the story.

Because we did not hear it from President Obama first, it somehow means that there is a cover up. President Obama addressed such claims saying, "Who executes some sort of cover up or effort to tamp things down for three days?"[24] In relation to the Benghazi attack, three days after they released information that it was the YouTube video that inspired the attack, they knew that it was actually in fact a preplanned attack. Why only keep the cover-up for three days, while also stating that the case is still developing, and then say what happened once the intelligence revealed it, if it was a cover-up? If anything, President Obama was being too transparent in giving information prematurely, instead of playing it closer to the chest and disclosing the details once he knew what happened. Of course then we would be talking about how he kept it a secret for three days.

Since people like comparisons so much, think about this one. We entered two wars under the premise that there were weapons of mass destruction. This was not a three-day "lie" if you can even call Obama's situation that. It was a prolonged excuse to get involved in a war that we never knew exactly why we were there. In fact the mission changed so much that we were basically picking names out of a hat at one point. "Operation Iraqi Freedom," "Operation New Dawn," a war for oil, "The War on Terror," and whatever other false motivations we used to occupy a country we still have not left. The problem in this situation is we were the ones not clear

---

[24] Carrie Dann, "Obama dismisses Benghazi talking points controversy as a 'slideshow,'" *NBC News,* http://firstread.nbcnews.com/ news/2013/05/13/18232152-obama-dismisses-benghazi-talking-points-controversy-as-a-sideshow?lite, date accessed 23 May 2013

about our motives. Instead of us not knowing why four Americans died in Benghazi and why they attacked us, we had no idea why we went into Iraq, when it was actually extremists in Afghanistan that attacked us on September 11th.

President Obama was reporting facts as they came to him, not making up new missions as he went along. And instead of a multibillion-dollar war lasting for over a decade, the Obama Administration itself revealed the truth merely three days later, and revealed what they knew as it was developing from the beginning. I hardly doubt President Bush conspired to have America attacked to enter Iraq (although that Michael Moore movie is pretty concerning). I only bring up the Bush example because we did not want to impeach President Bush. We went along with his lies and thought we were justified in our actions. We know now that they were lies and we did not have justification for entering the war in Iraq. People might say that two wrongs do not make a right and they absolutely do not. President Obama does not get a pass because President Bush had a bigger misstep than he did. However, what we do have is a country so willing to get rid of someone that they don't like that they are willing to tarnish his reputation and the future three years of his term because he said "act of terror" and not "act of terrorism"

Young people don't have the patience for such nonsense; just as the rest of the American people don't want our government wasting time on frivolous matters. Unless we forgot, the American people are the ones who vote them into office. While all the political pandering might make them feel better about their inaction and put up a smokescreen for issues as gun control to go away, or how we never have another attack on a consulate again so that people do not die. By the way, under Bush, there were 13 attacks on embassies killing a total of 112 people, 12 of them being Americans.[25]

I do not want to defend President Obama more than he should be defended. I do not want to attack him more than he should be attacked either. I do not want to bring up President Bush's incidents to detract from President Obama's blunders. There are enough smoke screens and accusations about cover-ups. I only want to be fair in my dealings with them all. If there is a legitimate cover-up that President Obama actively knew about, he should be punished, but let's not put the cart before the horse. An accusation is not an acquittal. People are so quick to form judgments without learning the facts that we are just as guilty of what we criticize President Obama for in the Benghazi attack scandal. He rushed to judgment and did not deliver the facts. As are we every time the "Breaking News" banner runs across a news channel. The only problem is we stop listening before the news anchor says, "This story is still developing." We immediately think people are guilty of everything and everything else is one big conspiracy to cheat the American people.

This chapter first talked about young people not being involved in political conversations, not having representation, and not having faith in our politicians.

[25] Shwetika Baijal, "13 Benghazis Happened Under President Bush and Fox News Said Nothing," *PolicyMic*, http://www.policymic.com/articles/40811/13-benghazis-happened-under-president-bush-and-fox-news-said-nothing, date accessed 25 May 2013

Everything that I just explained is exactly why we eventually just stop caring. Young people and old people are not so different in these instances. We get tired of the scandals and the fake news stories. The difference is we seem to get tired of them much faster. Not only that, we are not even given a voice to express our opinions. How many young people were interviewed, asked or brought on television to discuss these issues? How many young news reporters are there that discuss issues like these on a daily basis? Are old people saying that our opinions do not matter? Do we not have a stake in these problems like everyone else?

I do not want to create a divide in the American people because we really do not need anything else to separate us, and I for one do not think that there is much difference between young people and Generation X. However, we have a unique perspective that is rarely, to never given the light of day. Sure, the older people just fight and bicker, but at least they are given an arena to do so.

Chapter 9:
Illusion of Choice

The 2012 presidential election results brought about many different emotions. For Democrats it was a night of celebration. For Republicans it was a sad day of defeat. For everyone else...who am I kidding? There is no "everyone else." The whole country is either blue or red right? There is no shade of purple or teal or off red. This country is decidedly one or the other and if you are anything else, then you might as well move to a different country. More than that, if your blue team wins at the election then you get to gloat and shove it in the red team's face right? Wrong. But it must be true that when your team loses you get to pout and complain for the next for years about how the country is going to burn to the ground, right? Wrong. When we have an election and we elect a new president, there is no right or left, blue or red, or a divided nation. Well there is, but there shouldn't be. The American people exercised their right to vote and democracy wins. We have a president that represents us all no matter if he perfectly represents your every interest. It is impossible for one person to do that anyway.

When it comes to electing a president, what we have in this country is a dichotomized idea of democracy, which is ultimately an illusion of choice. You can either be blue or red. Anything else might as well not vote. This changed a bit in electing congress members with the introduction of the Tea Party, but more on them later. The reason why this has become an issue in this country as of late is because after President Obama was elected a second time, everyone wanted to get rid of the Electoral

College. Never mind that this was really political pouting because the right was upset they lost because the idea still holds some validity. If we are a democracy then how can we actually say that only a few swing states matter in every election? Ohio must be sick of presidential candidates frequenting their state every four years, and then never return once the election is over.

California is always going to vote democrat and it has since the 1990s. Why would republicans even vote in a state like this if their vote essentially does not even count? The other issue we should have with the Electoral College is that the winner is not always the winner. This was proven as recently as in the 2000 election where Al Gore won the popularity vote over President Bush. Gore received 48.4% of the vote, while President Bush only received 47.9%. However, instead of going with the American people, we rely on distributed point values allocated to different states based on population. So by these standards, President Bush won the election with 271 electoral votes over 266. Even when you have the most votes, the person does not win.

The reason why we have this process for voting presidents and vice presidents is the smaller states feared that the larger states would dominate elections. This however, makes no sense. A vote is a vote no matter where it is cast. The majority of people who all collectively agree should be able to decide. The votes in California do not get weighed more in a popular vote because one vote means one vote. In the Electoral College, not only do larger states get weighed more by having more electoral votes, but also elections end up being decided by a minority of states anyway. It does not matter that California has more electoral votes than

Hawaii because the election is decided before Hawaii gets to vote and it all rests on Ohio's shoulders.

The other problem we have with this whole blue and red debate is that if candidates did not tell people what they were (republican, democrat, or other) I am willing to bet the voter turnout would be very different. People would be forced to actually listen to the actual issues instead of voting along the party lines. Let's play a game. I am going to list the campaign platform of a candidate and see if you can guess whom this person's party is. The only omissions that were made were to not giveaway the secret. You should also refrain from looking at the footnotes because this will give away the secret as well (not that anyone reads footnotes).

On the economy, this presidential candidate wanted to:

> Maintain Fiscal Discipline and Eliminate the National Debt: ... We now have a historical opportunity to pay off the publicly held national debt. [This presidential candidate] believes we should use a large portion of the expected budget surplus to pay down our national debt. This fiscally-disciplined approach assures that our children will not be saddled with debt - and the enormous annual interest burden on that debt - and the costs of paying for the Baby Boomers' retirement. It assures that the United States will be debt free by 2012 - the first time since 1835. Paying down the publicly held debt will keep long-term interest rates low, allowing for greater investment in the private sector and bolstering

economic growth.[26]

Does this candidate sound familiar yet? The economy was such a big deal in the 2012 election that this should be a dead giveaway for whether you want to elect this person or not. I mean if you do not like this person's idea then you have no other choice but to vote for the other guy. If you like this person's idea then clearly you would have voted for him or her. Sounds like a pretty good idea to pay down the national debt, but you probably have not figured out whom the person is yet so let's continue.

On taxes:

> [This candidate] supports a pro-growth, pro-savings $500 billion package of targeted tax cuts and credits that fits within a responsible budget framework and helps working families - tax cuts to afford quality child care, higher education and lifelong learning, health insurance and long-term care for an aging or disabled relative. [This person] will also eliminate the marriage penalty for working families offering estate tax relief for small business owners and family farmers.[27]

Do you know who this is yet? Surely by now you know if you would have voted for this person. Maybe you are saying that it is not fair because you have nothing to judge this person against. Let's make it even easier to decide who is the best candidate (supposedly) and put

---

[26] 4Presidents, "Al Gore 2000 On The Issues," *4Presidents,* http://www.4president.us/issues/gore2000/gore2000econo my.htm, date accessed 12 May 2013

[27] ibid

what his or her opponent had to say about taxes so you can compare.

Opponent on taxes:

> "[This presidential candidate's] economic plan saves over half the surplus to strengthen Social Security and reduce the national debt, and saves over 10% of the surplus for important priorities like education, national defense and health. This still leaves a quarter of the surplus for much needed, long-overdue tax relief. [This person's] goal is to make it easier for people to join the middle class by cutting taxes and making them fairer. [This person's] tax cut will reduce tax rates for every taxpayer, double the child tax credit, slash the marriage penalty, expand deductions for charitable giving, make the research and development tax credit permanent and end the death tax. The biggest percentage reductions go to those in the lower tax brackets because they often face higher marginal tax rates than the wealthy. Taxpayers earning below $50,000, will see their income tax bills cut by over 20% on average. Some politicians say America cannot afford a tax cut in this time of prosperity. [This person] says if we leave the money in Washington, it will spent on more government and that giving it back to taxpayers through cuts and reforms is an important insurance policy to help guarantee continued prosperity."[28]

---

[28] 4Presidents, "George W. Bush for President 2000 Campaign Brochure" *4Presidents,* http://www.4president.org/brochures/georgewbush2000bro

This was a little longer than the first person on taxes, but they sound almost exactly the same: tax cuts for people making below $50,000, fairer tax laws, tax cuts so families can afford education, and restore the middle class.

Surely now you know clearly which candidate you would have voted for and it could not be more obvious. You probably don't even need it but let's use one more example, just to solidify your guess. Wars and foreign policy are always big at debates so let's see the first candidate's stance on the military, and then the opponent as we did above.

The candidate on the military:

> [This presidential candidate] believes the United States must remain actively engaged in the world through a strategy of Forward Engagement - addressing problems early in their development before they become crises, addressing them as close to the source of the problem as possible, and having the forces and resources to deal with those threats as soon after their emergence as possible. To support and sustain that strategy, America will have to maintain the best trained, best equipped, most agile military force in the world. As President, [this person] will devote part of the surplus to make reasonable increases in military spending - targeted to improve benefits and quality of life for servicemen and women, improve force readiness and provide the most

chure.htm, date accessed 12 May 2013

modern equipment. [This person] will also ensure adequate funding for an effective and secure foreign policy presence abroad, and address emerging security.[29]

Now his opponent:

[This candidate] believes America's military is challenged by aging weapons and failed intelligence. He will strengthen our military and rebuild America's stature in the world.

He will increase military pay $1 billion to raise morale and get military families off food stamps. He will improve military housing and allowances. He'll end shortfalls in training, spare parts, and equipment and modernize weapons and equipment. [This person] will defend Americans and our allies against missiles and blackmail by deploying an anti-ballistic missile defense. He will rebuild our intelligence services. As President [this person] will order an immediate review of overseas deployments: no U.S. troops should be in harm's way unless America's interests are at stake, no U.S. troops will ever serve under UN command.[30]

By now you definitely have your mind made up. You

---

[29] 4Presidents, "Al Gore 2000 On The Issues," *4Presidents,* http://www.4president.us/issues/gore2000/gore2000econo my.htm, date accessed 12 May 2013

[30] 4Presidents, "George W. Bush for President 2000 Campaign Brochure" *4Presidents,* http://www.4president.org/brochures/georgewbush2000bro chure.htm, date accessed 12 May 2013

know which guy is blue and which guy is red. You know whom you would pick and it would be the same person you picked in 2000. Oh! That was the first clue, so now you know one guy is Bush and one guy is Gore. Before I make the big reveal, let's look at the difference between the two ideas on foreign policy.

Both men want the best-trained and strongest military. Both men want better lives for those serving in the military. Both want better intelligence so we can better protect ourselves. Both want to give more money to the military. So surely one guy is an enemy and the other is a hero, right? And now the reveal. The first candidate was none other than Al Gore. That's right the candidate listed first each time was the person we did not elect. The person who was clearly the better candidate was the man we did choose: President George W. Bush. Did you get it right? If you did well then great, but I am not sure how you could have possibly distinguished between the two. It would have taken a very close eye to tell the difference between the two platforms. One giveaway is that Gore called for "Forward Engagement" instead of preemptive attacks. However, nowhere is the word "preemptive" in President Bush's campaign platform. The reason for this is because campaigning is very different than governing. On paper, these two men are not that different, but no one would have expected 9/11 to happen. In the media however, we paint them as polar opposites. We do this because it would not be interesting otherwise.

We can judge Bush more critically because he was actually elected so we can see if he kept to his promises. He did create tax breaks, but this ultimately torpedoed the country and created a massive debt. Do you know that debt that every republican likes to blame Obama for?

Did you know that it was actually Bush's policies and plans that would not kick in until Obama took office that actually sent the debt out of control? This will be a quick math problem to reveal the truth of the matter, but I do know that Americans often have problems with the math and truth so I will make it clear. President Obama was inaugurated on January 20, 2009. The Treasury Department has a debt to the penny website that tells the debt on any given date. On Obama's inauguration day, the debt was at $10.6 trillion. Funny how he could have increased the debt so much before he even took office. The debt is now 16.7 trillion, which is from the time Obama took office until now.

Of course everyone can now say well Obama increased the debt more in four years than Bush did in 8 years. This is only true because the Bush administration played hot potato with the debt and Obama was left to pay for two wars that President Bush used borrowed money to fund. Granted, President Obama did not cool down the potato, as it started to burn a whole in our country only digging us deeper and deeper into debt. Before you think this is just a tangent, it was actually a great example in how our country's divisions are not accurate. President Obama increased the debt. President Bush increased the debt. In fact, President Obama would be the most republican of all recent presidents because increasing the debt has been an unfortunate republican tradition since Ronald Reagan. The only time the debt was decreased and we had a surplus was when there was a democrat – Bill Clinton. There is no blue America or a red America. It is often almost impossible to distinguish one person from another. The fact that we are only given two choices though is absurd.

There are some issues that anyone can agree with a candidate on and some people will disagree on. There is not one candidate that can fully capture a whole electorate. We try to say that there is by pitting one guy against another guy claiming that every American either likes A or like B. This is just laughably not the case and also why young people grow disinterested in politics. The constant bickering and putting one against another does not promote democracy. It just creates a circus with the media as ringleaders.

We want a candidate who stands for our principles and is not going to go back on his or her word once he or she is elected. This is essentially the problem with campaigning. It was almost impossible to tell Gore from President Bush because of course their speeches and statements are going to sound very pro-American and vague. Providing too many details means you actually have to hold to your promise. So what it boils down to is a popularity contest anyway. Who do we like the best? Who do we want to go have a beer with? If this is the case, then why not elect the right person based on popularity? This is something old people can learn from young people. Popularity contests are what we know best. We are often not that far removed from high school so these kinds of things are in our wheelhouses.

It should be, but this is a level of childishness that we can no longer tolerate. We grow impatient of the bickering and squabbling that does not lead to productive conversations. Quite frankly, we just want the best candidate in office that is going to help move forward an American agenda – not a democratic or republican one. People say there are more than two candidates all the time and people can vote from a number of different people other than republicans and democrats. If that is the case, then why aren't these candidates involved in the debates? Why are they not allowed to voice their opinions on a grand scale as the two big parties? We cannot say that they are not big enough or not established enough to be seen as actual legitimate parties because the reason they are so small is because they do not get national recognition. I know, a catch 22. Should the American people only be force fed two seemingly opposing ideas? Is it that Americans only have the attention span to focus on two candidates? Is it much easier for the media to attack one and promote another without all the other candidates getting in the way?

People need to listen to what they are voting for instead of sticking to party lines. Democrats and republicans both will vote against their personal interests just to align with a party. If people want to vote Republican because of religious reasons that is their prerogative and the reason why we have a democracy. Just make sure you are listening to the candidates when they talk. Make sure their social policies do not cripple you economically and otherwise. There is a culture of "they aren't talking about me" but they actually are. Mitt Romney infamously called out the 47% of Americans that are takers. A little less than half of the company he referred to as dependent and users. The fact that there was even still a close race at that point speaks volumes about this country. If we are willing to vote for a president that says he does not speak for 47 percent of this country, when the President of the United States must speak for us all, we will vote for anyone who says anything merely because they are the nominee for the democratic or republican party. We don't care what they say, but as long as they wear a blue tie or a red tie, we like them.

In case anyone forgot what Romney said exactly (as if that is possible after MSNBC replayed it a million times, let's put it in print.

> "There are 47 percent of the people who will vote for the president no matter what ... who are dependent upon government, who believe that they are victims. ... These are people who pay no income tax. ... and so my job is not to worry about those people. I'll never convince them that they should take personal responsibility and care for their lives"[31]

Interestingly enough, Romney and I are saying a very similar thing. I want to make very clear now that I do not believe democrats think they are "victims" who do not know how to "take personal responsibility and care for their lives." The only thing we agree on is about 47 percent of this country are democrats so he is right in not having to "worry about those people" because they are going to vote democrat "no matter what." There is probably an equal 47 percent of this country that is going to vote republican. All that is left that all presidential candidates then fight over is the last six percent of this country who are the swing voters. Although a very divisive and a toxic thing to say for a man who does not want to be elitist, with our current two party system, Mitt Romney was correct. It could have been said in a more elegant manner, but when you are behind closed doors,

---

[31] John Christoffersen, "Romney's '47 percent' chosen as year's best quote," *Associated Press*, http://news.yahoo.com/romneys-47-percent-chosen-years-best-quote-162127619.html, date accessed 27 May 2013

why let flowery words get in the way of how you really feel.

Mitt Romney's gaff could not have been more damaging, as it should have been because it was a very foolish thing to say about the country. At its very core and premise though he is speaking to a problem in this country where we only have two sides. There is no convincing a republican to vote democrat, or convincing a democrat to vote republican. We bleed either blue or red until we die. Of course there is a very small number of people who change cotes, but I am not talking about them and neither was Romney. Those are the swing voters that presidents must appeal to. I am talking about the devout political loyalists who can never be swayed one way or another. The interesting thing though is we often want the same exact outcomes from the president we elect. There are issues universal to us all.

Here are some things that do not have a political color attached to them or do not abide by any party principle.

1. America is ranked 17th in education as compared to other developed nations.[32]

2. The debt in America has amassed to $16.7 trillion.[33]

[32] Huffington Post, "Best Education In The World: Finland, South Korea Top Country Rankings, U.S. Rated Average," *Huffington Post,* http://www.huffingtonpost.com/2012/11/27/best-education-in-the-wor_n_2199795.html, date accessed 26 May 2013

[33] Romina Boccia, "Washington Hits the $16.7 Trillion Debt Ceiling with $300 Billion in New Debt," *The*

3. American unemployment rate is at 7.5%.[34]

4. 15.7% of Americans are uninsured.[35]

5. Everyday 289 people in this country are shot and everyday 86 of them die from guns.[36]

6. The U.S. makes up only 5% of the world's populations, yet we are responsible for 22 percent of the world's carbon emissions.[37]

Foundry, http://blog.heritage.org/2013/05/19/washington-hits-the-16-7-trillion-debt-ceiling-with-300-billion-in-new-debt/, 22 May 2013

[34] James Pethokoukis, "Is the real US unemployment rate 11.3% or 7.5%? A new Goldman Sachs study offers an answer," *AEI Ideas,* http://www.aei-ideas.org/2013/05/is-the-real-us-unemployment-rate-11-3-or-7-5-a-new-goldman-sachs-study-offers-an-answer/, date accessed 4 June 2013

[35] Susan R. Todd and Benjamin D. Sommers, "Overview of the Uninsured in the United States: A Summary of the 2012 Current Population Survey Report," *ASPE,* http://aspe.hhs.gov/health/reports/2012/uninsuredintheus/ib.shtml, date accessed 24 May 2013

[36] Kevork Djansezian, "Just the facts: Gun violence in America," *NBC News,* http://usnews.nbcnews.com/_news/2013/01/16/16547690-just-the-facts-gun-violence-in-america?lite

[37] The Nature Conservancy, "Climate Change: Facts about Climate Change," *The Nature Conservancy,* http://www.nature.org/ourinitiatives/urgentissues/global-warming-climate-change/help/facts-about-climate-change.xml, date accessed 22 May 2013

7. The top one percent of the country owns 43 percent of the wealth.[38]

8. The top one percent of the country owns 43 percent of the wealth.

   a. Repeating this was not an error. It was to highlight a point in case you missed it.

9. The top five percent of the country controls 72 percent of the wealth.[39]

10. 250 members of Congress are millionaires.[40]

11. 11 percent of congress is part of the financial elite.[41]

Did any of these things make you angry or at least give you pause? If they did then there is something that should be done in this country and we are not done fighting for progress. How can we expect our elected officials to do anything about poverty, or the economy when they are millionaires? They might be representatives, but they only represent a small minority of very wealthy people in this country. These issues are not supposed to be in line with any one political party.

---

[38] Alan Dunn, "Average America vs the One Percent," *Forbes*, http://www.forbes.com/sites/moneywisewomen/2012/03/21/average-america-vs-the-one-percent/, 22 May 2013

[39] ibid

[40] ibid

[41] ibid

These are issues that all of us as Americans and living in this country face, whether we like it or not. We can beat our chests and talk about how one party is better than another, but neither party has fixed the list of problems above. This is not even close to an exhaustive list of problems this country faces, but this should be enough to make anyone see that there are injustices that we all face.

If you imagine yourself in the top 5% then you are probably delusional. Even if you actually are, do you really think it is fair that there are people who cannot afford to eat while you have caviar on your private jet? Of course rich people "worked" to get to where they are, but there are people working and cannot afford to feed their families. So the next time you hear someone say that this country has too many takers ask them if they are referring to the one percent of this country who only pays 18 percent in taxes from their person income, while the people in the 15 percent tax bracket pay 30 percent of the total taxes collected in this country. Of course the top one percent pays more in taxes than everyone else because they make gargantuan amounts of money.

The faux middle class that we have today like to say that they pay their fair share of taxes and it is the takers at the bottom who do not work and mooch off everyone else that are ruining this country. After all, only 53 percent of this country pays taxes and the other 47 percent are takers right? Let's look at the numbers. Even when the country is fully employed, as it was in 2007, only 40 percent of the country did not pay federal income taxes. This whole not paying taxes thing is usual because you have to look deeply into the numbers.

Of those who do not pay income tax, 60 percent of them

are still working. They just do not make enough money to even qualify to pay federal income tax. Another 22 percent of those people are your grandparents who are retired. That's right, 22 percent of the people lumped into the takers category not paying federal income taxes are retired. So 82 percent of people who are mooching, are either still working and don't make enough money to qualify to pay federal income taxes, let alone provide for their families, or once worked to provide a life for you and are now retired. It is actually only 7.9 percent of households that do not pay taxes and do not work – which also includes groups of people as those on disability and students.[42]

So the measly amount of taxes you are paying isn't being spread so thin that you are supporting the lives of a bunch of moochers in this country. The people you should be looking at as takers for taking too much and not giving enough are the very rich – you know, those people you do not want to blame because you hold out hope you will become them one day. And that is really the crux of this issue. The middle class aspires to climb the social ladder and feel like in order to get there, they must distance themselves from the poor as much as they can, instead of realizing that the only wealth gap they should care about is between the top five percent and everyone else in the country. Those are the people we should all have a problem with. The real divide that is hurting this country is the one between the rich and the

[42] Brad Plumer, "Who doesn't pay taxes, in eight charts," *Washington Post*, http://www.washingtonpost.com/blogs/wonkblog/wp/2012/09/18/who-doesnt-pay-taxes-in-charts/, date accessed 24 May 2013

poor, but somehow we are more distracted by the red and blue debate.

Young people fit in this situation quite nicely because they have an opportunity to ignore their parents and the generations of familial party lines to enter the election debates with fresh eyes and ears. They do not have to just fall in line and become a sheep for the cause. As first time voters, they have an opportunity to listen to a candidate for whom he or she is without prejudice or bias.

This can even be hard at times because sometimes a candidate is not even really what they appear to be.

I am not picking on Romney, but he provides a perfect example for the flaws that exist in our electoral system. His senior campaign advisor, Eric Fehrnstrom, when asked about Romney having to change his stance on different issues, claimed, "I think you hit a reset button for the fall campaign. Everything changes. It's almost like an Etch A Sketch. You can kind of shake it up, and we start all over again."[43] So forget everything you said when running in the primaries because that does not matter anymore. Forget about having principles and not being an actual republican when you were running in the republican primary. Forget about having such radical ideas that even the average republican could not stomach. Forget about all that because once you get elected to be the republican nominee, you will magically

---

[43] Tom Cohen, "Romney's big day marred by Etch A Sketch remark," *CNN*, http://www.cnn.com/2012/03/21/politics/campaign-wrap, 30 May 2013

transform into a red blooded man with a red glow and here to serve these united states of the red, red, and red.

Immediately you become someone you are not once you have that democratic or republican moniker behind you. You adopt ideas that you think will get you elected instead of ideas you actually believe in. You merely fall in line with a party instead of thinking about what is best for this country. The reason why I have not yet picked on President Obama for doing something very similar is because I have a section dedicated to Mr. Blue. Stay tuned.

Chapter 10:
One Term of Greatness or Two Terms of Mediocrity?

Unfortunately in this country a president's success is measured not by what they get done, but if they are reelected. The reason why Generation Y should take offense to this is because we came out in the largest numbers in history to support a president who did not entirely live up to his end of the bargain. 2008 Obama was a man that inspired passion and hope in young people. He spoke with eloquence like no one we have ever seen in our short lifetimes. He invigorated a generation to believe that politics was not filled with corruption, greed and party dedications. He seemed as if he were a beacon of hope for anyone dreaming to have something better in this country than what they had. President Obama should have been a great one-term president instead of a mediocre two-term president.

Has Obama done great things in this country? Sure he has. He has instituted healthcare reform that has long been needed in this country and many repealed. The economy is turning around (slowly) but it is moving. We have an end date for the wars we were thrust into. Don't ask don't tell was repealed, he killed Osama bin Laden (not himself, but you get the idea), and he restored a certain level of respect America had in the eyes of international leaders. Unfortunately, no matter what he has done, he will always be judged for what he did not do. The economy is not completely back to Clinton era success. Gay marriage is still not legal for the nation. Guantanamo Bay is still up and running. Immigration reform, education reform, gender inequalities, and a mountain of other issues are still sitting on his desk.

Although he has three more years until he must move out of the White House, the hope that change can actually be made is something that has dwindled significantly amongst young people and Americans all over the country.

Now, the reason for this loss of hope is not entirely his fault. The deadlocked congress that we have has ultimately shined a spotlight on the chaos that is politics. No matter how much President Obama tries to play nice and live up to one of the greatest American principles – compromise – he will be blamed for not reaching across the aisle. Hindsight is 20/20, but what Americans were looking for when they voted for him was someone that was going to come in and institute some of his ideas because, well, they elected him. I know that is a crazy thought, but when majority of the American people like what he has to say and like his ideas enough to vote for him, they want some of those ideas to actually be implemented. Yet here we are and Guantanamo Bay is not yet closed. As this is written, President Obama is revisiting this issue and asking for its closure again, yet we continue to rely on congress to push it through. Let's get very real right now: congress will wait him out and not do a thing as long as he is president. There will be nothing that democrats will be able to tout as success in the coming 2016 election.

Unfortunately for Hilary Clinton or Joe Biden, they will actually have to distinguish themselves from President Obama. They will not have to do it because of any of his flaws or will not have to run from him as McCain tried to distance himself from President Bush, but they will have to explain why they will be able to get things done. They will not get to run on mounting success and claim they can continue the valiant efforts, despite them actually being valiant efforts. History can judge President Obama's success very differently, but currently what we have is a president who is not viewed as someone who enacted change quick enough. Understandably dealing with congress is like dealing with a child who will not stop crying. Either you let her cry until she has wore herself out and you both go about your day exhausted, or you give in. President Obama refuses to give in because the ideas on the other side are not what the majority of Americans want, so we end up with a bunch of elected officials sucking their thumbs and cuddled up next to their teddy bears getting ready to take a nap.

Now there was a time when President Obama essentially owned all parts of congress. From the House to the Senate, he could have basically done anything he wanted. Americans were ready for change and were almost desperate for it after eight years of the Bush Administration, so they elected a majority of democrats for all parts of our government. Somehow healthcare became the first monster that took up all of our time. With talks about death panels and the government hands intruding in our Medicare, the country was distracted long enough to let Republicans take over the House of Representatives. After that this whole supermajority thing was cemented into place, essentially killing any bill before it is even dreamt up. For two years Obama almost had a free pass to address any issue he wanted. The whole talk of Obama's first 100 days had people hoping that something monumental was going to happen, and it was going to happen quickly. Instead, Americans, and especially young Americans, were left waiting at the alter.

This is a great time to remind you about the caveat I set in the beginning of this book that when I say "especially young people" I am not suggesting young people are more deserving of anything. President Obama did not have a special contract with young people over other generations, but the reason why this election was special is because young people came out in droves like never before. This being the case, there was a whole new group of people that were let down with the slowness that change is implemented. Because of this, and the fact that crap rolls down hill, the impossible to overcome divisions that started out in congress have found their way to the American people.

This is where I turn the tables on us all because we are all just as responsible for whatever did not happen that we wanted to happen so quickly. We had unrealistic expectations for ourselves and what change actually meant. Remember that President Obama did not win 100% of the electorate so there was and is still an opposition that he has to listen to. We elect presidents, not dictators, and because of that he could not just swoop in, slap republicans around and enact changes. If anything else, President Obama is a predictor of his own demise. In his first election speech in 2008 he addressed almost exactly what happened to the American people and tried to warn them against such an inevitable future. Apparently many people have forgotten what he said not too long ago, so let me remind you:

> "This victory alone is not the change we seek. It is only the chance for us to make that change. And that cannot happen if we go back to the way things were. It can't happen without you, without a new spirit of service, a new spirit of sacrifice.

118

So let us summon a new spirit of patriotism, of responsibility, where each of us resolves to pitch in and work harder and look after not only ourselves but each other."

And the crux of it all - what newly elected President Obama said only a few lines before those above:

"The road ahead will be long. Our climb will be steep. We may not get there in one year or even in one term. But, America, I have never been more hopeful than I am tonight that we will get there."[44]

Somewhere we forgot everything he said back in 2008. We forgot that we play a part in his work and the work of our government beyond just electing them all. We forgot that change does not come as fast as we can send a tweet. The American people merely elected President Obama to get a change in focus. His election only readjusted the needle and pointed it in a different direction. It would take more than just him to move the needle toward the change that people sought after. It was not going to happen in the first 100 days, as people had hoped for. Remember, we wanted a lot of change. We didn't just want a few things to be altered here and there. We wanted massive overhauls. We wanted to end two wars without starting another. We wanted to come out of an economy on the brink of disaster. We wanted social changes that had never been fought for before. Will "we get there" and will we ever see these changes we thought

---

[44] CNN, "Transcript: 'This is your victory,' says Obama," *CNN*, http://edition.cnn.com/2008/POLITICS/11/04/obama.transcript/, date accessed 1 June 2013

President Obama was going to enact? Well we should know better than anyone else. President Obama might be able to predict the future, but we have the power to actually do something about it. We can make the changes we want to see made, but there must be enough passion and drive in our hearts to get something done. No matter if you are red or blue, as President Obama said in 2008, "What began 21 months ago in the depths of winter cannot end on this autumn night."

Unfortunately what began years ago did die on that autumn night in 2008. People forgot that a president is only as strong as the people who elected him or her. This country became so exhausted with celebrating his win that they decided to take off the next four years. It was like he was leading a charge. He said all the right things, got people all fired up and then when he was ready to run forward for change, everyone else stayed in place. What he ran into was a Tea Party armed with a filibuster and a congress unwilling to reason. The American people left President Obama to be a one-man revolution and when he needed them the most, they claimed he was not moving fast enough. It is true from the outside looking in it appeared that he was enjoying his tour of the White House too much before he actually saw the issues on his desk. Nevertheless, I am sure that as president, red or blue, the country is always the first priority. In our everyday dealings the country is probably in the backdrop of our lives. In the day of the life of an American civilian, we are just trying not to get fired from our jobs and make it to the weekend. The president has a responsibility greater than most of us know, but that comes with the job. He is not pardoned from criticism and we can all expect certain things from him or her. Nevertheless, what we must be is realistic in our expectations.

The political climate is very different in 2013 than it was in 2009 when President Obama first took office. He does not have the same liberties he had with a democratic Congress and his naïveté that people would actually work with him is gone. So how do you work in an environment where no one is willing to budge on an issue? How can you get anything accomplished when everyone is simply going to stick to party lines? The simple answer is you cannot. However, that is where the frustration within me boils. How can we simply stand and watch as a country gets held hostage by politics. When do we stop treating the president as a figurehead for which we can blame success or failures on and become accountable for our own inaction? If we want something done, it is going to take more than signing a petition on change.org. President Obama is one branch of a government that has checks and balances that prevent government overreach. This being the case, when there is a deadlock among the people signing the legislation we must be the tiebreaker. We must express our concern with the problems this country faces.

President Obama could have been a one-term president that got things done, but no one liked. Instead, he became a two-term president that people are waiting on to get things done. Forget what he said about change not coming fast. Forget about what he said about needing the help of all this country's citizens to get change accomplished. Forget actually investing more time into this country than simply voting. We (myself included) are victims only as long as we make ourselves out to be victims. We can sit by idly and become the passive onlookers for social change that President Obama warned against, or we can actually join the debate and disregard party politics to put the country first. Since you like voting so much, decide which it will be.

Chapter 11:
You are Invited to a Tea Party

We talk about the two party system, but suddenly this might not be the case for too long. There used to be a libertarian party in this country where people wanted to focus on the individual liberties that we all should possess. This stems from a political freedom where government should be hands off. Instead of being neither republican nor democrat, this party has transformed into some ultraconservative party we all know now as the Tea Party. Although at first a punch line on most late night talk shows, the Tea Party has divided the Republican Party and has built a lasting base that will not be ignored.

The reason why I give the Tea Party any credit in reference to a book addressing young people is because this grass roots movement teaches us all a lesson. People who are angry enough will eventually all band together and focus their anger into some collective form of protest. What we have learned though is either they can be a productive mass moving for the betterment of society, as with the Civil Rights movements or the Arab Spring, or it can create the Tea Party. I think the Tea Party, as a movement, is a perfect demonstration for how people should unite together to enact changes they believe in. I just do not believe in their changes, and neither do many young people, and just people in general. In case you do not know what they stand for I will tell you.

This list below comes from the Tea Party website and the

title of it is "15 Non-negotiable Core Beliefs"[45]

1. Illegal aliens are here illegally.
2. Pro-domestic employment is indispensable.
3. A strong military is essential.
4. Special interests must be eliminated.
5. Gun ownership is sacred.
6. Government must be downsized.
7. The national budget must be balanced.
8. Deficit spending must end.
9. Bailout and stimulus plans are illegal.
10. Reducing personal income taxes is a must.
11. Reducing business income taxes is mandatory.
12. Political offices must be available to average citizens.
13. Intrusive government must be stopped.
14. English as our core language is required.
15. Traditional family values are encouraged.

Let us first clear what is okay with this list. Of course this country will always and forever have a strong military, as ours surpasses most countries combined, so belief three is stating the obvious. It goes without saying that the budget should be balanced and congress should be punished for not getting budgets passed without political pandering. Jobs should be focused in this country so there is nothing wrong with the second idea. Political offices are available to average citizens so number 12 is ridiculous and just affirmation of what already is the case. If we are just stating things that are not even questioned, why not put on the list that the sky

---

[45] Tea Party, "About Us, *Tea Party*, http://www.teaparty.org/about-us/, date accessed 21 May 2013

is blue and the president must be a human being? Number four is a great standard for our government and special interests should have no place in our government. Other than these, all of the others are up for debate.

And therein lies the first problem of this list.

The first problem is not even in the list itself, but the name of the list. The fact that these mandates or "beliefs" are "non-negotiable" suggests that the Tea Party is unwilling to compromise. As a political party, it cannot be the framework of the people that they will not budge on any of these issues. As vague as they are, it is pretty all encompassing, not allowing for any change whatsoever. Now I think I am starting to get their point. (Sarcasm is not easily expressed in text, but that last sentence was sarcastic). Of course they do not want change because that would disrupt the status quo of this country. In describing how the Tea Party movement started, the website declares, "We were more than lowly protestors; we were the type of Americans the Founding Fathers envisioned over 200 years ago as true Patriots of courage and valor."[46] This statement at its core completely contradicts everything the founding fathers stood for and was not what they envisioned, as a party starts taking over the country. They wanted a political process filled with compromise and open-mindedness. This is why we have a democracy. If the American people have a list of beliefs that we must all agree to before entering a conversation than we are not promoting open discussion. What we are promoting is singular thinking and this goes against everything American. This country is made up of different races, religions, belief

_____

[46] ibid.

systems, and ideas. Having to conform to one set of ideas created by a few is an oligarchic nation and not a democratic one.

Moreover, the movement contradicts what the Founding Fathers imagined for this country in the very list of rules they set forth, especially in number 6 where they believe the government must be downsized. The Constitution was made in order to make the central government bigger because the "Founding Fathers" believed that states had too much power distributed across them without a centralized government. There should not be an "intrusive" government as they state, but that word has gone on to take on new meaning. Trying to regulate guns has been called "intrusive." Intrusion is entering homes and telling people whom they should marry or telling people if they can use contraception, or if they can get an abortion. Ironically and a complete contradiction, traditional family values would enter into the realm of intrusion when people start telling you how to live in your home.

What is surprising is that for a people who were intelligent enough to build this party that will not go away, despite even Republican's best efforts, the people in it do not know arithmetic. Reducing business and individual taxes will not bring in enough money for this country to prosper. We have a deficit. If we merely stop spending, it is not going to bring in new revenue. We will still have a deficit. Think about the country as your home. If today, I told you to just stop spending so much money in your house, but then I also told you to quit your job, you would think I was crazy. How would you sustain your lifestyle? How would you bring in money to support your family? The math works the same for a family of five, as it does for an entire nation. If they want a balanced budget, the people who are making disproportionate amounts of money in this country are going to have to pay their fair share. We need taxes. The original "tea baggers" (not those so get your mind out of the gutter) the ones involved in the Boston Tea Party were fighting because they claimed that there would be "No taxation without representation." Conservatives seem to have a problem with looking at the whole sentence of things because this is the same debate that is constantly had with the second amendment. Just like you have a right to a gun to form a militia, the colonists in 1773 were fighting the fact that they were being taxed, *but not directly represented by the British Parliament*. So if the British Parliament decided to pass laws as the Sugar Act, the British Americans had no say in the matter because they had no representation, or a voice in the government. They were not saying that the government should reduce taxes, which is what this revamped Tea Party wants in a time where the country needs help the most. I will grant anyone the point that businesses should not get as many tax exemptions as they do and they should not be able to get around taxes with a plethora of loopholes that the average citizen is not privy to, but they must pay taxes.

If this is their faux-constitution, then it is contradictory to the core of this country that they frequently use as their evidence for preventing any progressive change in this country. With belief number 14 that English is the core language suggests that immigrants and their native languages are unwelcome. This is solidified in the first rule that illegal immigrants are here illegally. Despite the redundancy in the first belief, it is clear they want immigration controlled, if not rid of altogether. Although there should be immigration reform, cutting it off completely, denying people their native language and forcing English upon them is not how we embrace different cultures, which is how this country was formed. Interestingly it is not until Republicans and Tea Party candidates realized that they cannot win elections without minority voters, they start to change their tune on immigration reform.

I am willing to have a conversation about these issues that they are not willing to negotiate on. I am also willing to give this radical party of extreme conservatives credit when it is due. The greatest thing I can say about the Tea Party is that they exist. Young people need to take a lesson in this grass roots movement that sprung up out of sheer hatred for Obama, I mean anger for our political direction. We are just as angry (I think) about the direction this country is heading towards, mostly because of the Tea Party. The Occupy movement was a complete disappointment, but not led by young people. What is more disappointing is there is no movement led by young people. We sit idly in our parents' homes sending out job applications hoping that Bill Gates will call us.

The Tea Party organized and came together for a common cause. At first the party was a little fragmented, as they were not entirely united other than their absolute detestation for the Obama administration. Then they started to rally behind the healthcare debate and this was enough fuel to the anti-government fire, encapsulating the libertarians and enough of the Republican Party to keep them from winning elections, as they spread across the country. For a political movement to exist in this country and for it to be done by a majority of older people with forty percent of them being 55 or older, shows that social media is not the end all be all to political action. Only 22 percent of Tea Party members are under 35. This means that 78 percent of tea baggers are old people. Sometimes it takes an old-fashioned approach to achieve organized success because in most dealings I have had with old people and technology, I am normally the one who walks away tired and frustrated.

If a party like this can make such a lasting impression on the way this government is run, basically holding any kind of change this country needs hostage, then there is something to be learned in their methods. The interesting part, and possibly the part that young people have trouble with is it did not involve a new fangled gadget to accomplish. Technology is great and I think improvements are great, but in a country where we swear complete allegiance to a 200-year-old document we call the Constitution, we are going to have to use older methods of inciting action and change. Some things are not going to be improved upon and virtual sit-ins and protests in the form of holograms are not going to change the course of our country.

Remember young people; it is the old people who run this country. They are not impressed when it comes to twitter because they mostly do not understand it. They do not care about the Facebook event that you created to rally support for a cause because they are mostly confused by the whole idea of a Facebook event. "Does the event actually happen on Facebook?" They are not interested in a trending hashtag for #occupywallstreet because the hashtag is still a pound sign on a telephone to them. We are going to have to meet them on their level and do not take this as an insult to anyone. We are not coming down to their level, nor should old people "rise to the occasion" of technology (well they should so they leave the innocent "Geniuses" at the Apple store alone) but there is no hierarchy here. There is just what works and what does not work. We have to recognize, as a country and as a generation that old school forms of organization and protest are far more effective than the social media exploits that have been tried. Social media can be a tool to drive these protests, but they cannot be the end all be all to social change. If we wait for the world to change then we will be waiting for a while because as we have all seen, change happens slowly. It is not going to keep up with the "I want it now" generation that we have grown accustomed to in the past few decades.

Although we should learn how effective the Tea Party was in forming, what we cannot be is what the Tea Party stands for in their dealings with this country. As a generation, we must be willing to negotiate and enter conversations that we never had before. Unfortunately that means having an actual conversation and not participating in a Facebook thread on your stoner friend's profile that he initiated trying to stir up trouble among his friends. We cannot think that our principles are so resolute that by merely listening to the opinion of another person we are betraying ourselves. We are actually doing what this country cherishes most and that is accepting other people's beliefs. Being steadfast in your opinions does not mean denying another perspective.

The Tea Party has made a name for itself, and although that is not a name that even many Republicans want to be associated with, it has proven that not all hope is lost for unity. They just united for causes you may not believe in, which is fine. The point is they united.

Chapter 12:
An Impossible Task: The Nation Today As Told By Our Constitution

What does a "more perfect Union" mean today? Are we perfect already? When the Constitution was made, the makers of a nation tried to answer this tough question. Little did they know that many, many years later, their standards would be the litmus test still seen as the benchmark for a perfect union today. Why have we tried to stop perfecting the country that many died to build?

In the very first section of the very first article of the Constitution it claims that, "All legislative Powers herein granted shall be vested in a Congress of the United States." Although a good idea at the time, the makers of the document could not have predicted the lack of unity we have today. Congress has been hijacked by a supermajority and threats of filibusters. I understand that this country has an arithmetic problem (only ranking 25th in mathematics for 15 year old students[47]), but when did majority stop meaning 51%? When democracy becomes redefined that 60% of people have to agree on something in order to get something accomplished, we have forsaken the ideas that the American people can make decisions. The House of Representatives and the Senate get to make up their own rules when deciding on how votes and discussions will work on the House and Senate

---

[47] Chung Sung-Jun, "In Ranking, U.S. students trail global leaders," *USA Today*, http://usatoday30.usatoday.com/news/education/2010-12-07-us-students-international-ranking_N.htm, date accessed 29 May 2013

floor – not the American people. This is actually the rule for congress. They can make up their own rules, thus we have a supermajority.

Young people do not have to be told or did not have to grow up hearing that the government is something we should be wary of trusting, as President Obama suggested in his commencement speech in Ohio because we can see it for ourselves. The schoolyard form of government we have is being left in shambles as it becomes harder for people to trust in the system that wants desperately to think of it as more than just a "sham," but is constantly reaffirmed in this premise. To give another example, and please forgive this moment of complete informality, but the filibuster has to be the most inane and juvenile form of governing we have fully embraced as a nation.

Imagine two kids playing a game of basketball after school and they are arguing about a foul one kid has made on the court. One kid says I am going to sit here and talk until the other gives up and doesn't want to argue anymore. The other kid says "Fine. I am just going to take my ball and go home." Was anything solved in this hypothetical situation with the two kids? Not at all. What did happen though is both sides walked away thinking they won. The arguing kid felt like the other kid gave up, so he must have been right. The kid who took the ball feels like he had complete control over the situation because he owned the ball to begin with so he had leverage on his side. Instead, the entire game was stopped, all because two people couldn't come to some kind of compromise.

This is the kind of behavior we expect from children, but

not the people making decisions about our livelihoods. In today's political climate, people do not even have to use the filibuster to incite fear in the eyes of an opponent. All it takes is a mere threat of a filibuster and legislation goes to die. Since Congress is so accepting of ridiculous ideas and style of governing, I propose a new filibuster – one that requires members of congress to not leave their seats until a deal or compromise is reached on legislation that comes across their eyes. If people want to talk for hours, then they have to talk about the issues at hand and not read the full Harry Potter series. If we are going to have lengthy conversations then they should be productive.

Political debate is healthy for any country but political pandering is an evil embedded in a government system that is ruled by special interests, which is ruled by money. Since people like capitalism so much, the government is really no different than a large corporation. The citizens are stockholders with a percentage of the company that means absolutely nothing at all. We just benefit or suffer from the choices of those we elect. Any decision that a single person or department wants to make has to be approved and if one or two guys up the ladder don't like an idea, it never happens. Companies talk about innovation and staying ahead of the competition using "21st century" techniques, when they are really not doing anything different than they had been doing since they started. This could be no truer when it comes to our government, especially when it comes to that oh so sacred document known as the U.S. Constitution.

We are bound by a document written over 200 years ago that is written for interpretation, thereby acting more as guidelines than hard fast rules to live by. A Constitution rewrite is not out of question. Before you stop reading and think, "oh this is just another radical liberal brainwashed by the mainstream media" understand that the Constitution that we hold so dear to our hearts is not the first one the United States has lived by. In 1777 the Continental Congress adopted the Articles of Confederation, which became fully ratified by the thirteen states existing at the time in 1781. This "constitution" was apparently too weak in terms of the role of the central government, giving too much power to the states (see that Tea Party). There was a need for a stronger federal government so the Constitutional Convention was held in 1787 to rewrite the original "binding" laws of the land. Our present day Constitution then replaced the Articles of Confederation in 1789. Despite all those *pesky* amendments like giving minorities and women rights, we have a document that many want unchanged forever.

As I just stated, the Constitution is meant, and was written to be revised. This is why we have amendments, which are granted in Article V of the document. Nevertheless, it is 2013 as this book is being written and the last amendment that was ratified was in 1992. In 21 years, the Constitution has not been updated, even though the people who wrote the first Articles of Confederation did a complete rewrite to the framework of this nation only 10 years later. In 200 years we have never done a rewrite. The ten most sacred of the amendments – the Bill of Rights – was ratified in 1791. We have lived by these "rights" for 222 years now and I constantly hear how this is a testament to the genius of our forefathers who could construct a document that resonates with us today. There is only one problem with that idea – the document does not resonate with us today.

I am not just attacking the Constitution or the Bill of Rights. I think there is a reason for tradition and it should be celebrated. That being said, it should not hold us hostage. Let's look at some of these bills – in their entirety. You cannot talk about the Bill of Rights without talking about the first amendment and the granddaddy of them all – the one that allows me to write such a book without facing some kind of punishment.

The first amendment states:

> "Congress shall make no law respecting an establishment of religion, or prohibiting the free exercise thereof; or abridging the freedom of speech, or of the press; or the right of the people peaceably to assemble, and to petition the Government for a redress of grievances."

I am a proponent of free speech, religion (separated from state), and everything encompassed in the amendment. That being said, there is no way that the forefathers could have foreseen the Internet when they drafted this document. I say that because with the anonymity that people have to hide behind their keyboard, there is a problem with accountability. The government cannot police the Internet, despite their best efforts, but just as we have the right to face our accusers in open court (amendment 6), people cannot say whatever they want anyone without having to take responsibility. The press used to be a reputable source for the news, but now that anyone can own a blog or a Twitter account, so many lies are spread that ruin careers, families, and people's lives.

Speaking to the point of ruining lives, the second amendment is next on our list.

The second amendment is as follows:

> "A well regulated Militia, being necessary to the security of a free State, the right of the people to keep and bear Arms, shall not be infringed."

Despite what the Supreme Court ruled on this amendment, which we will get to in a second, let's examine this one as it is. The amendment starts with the call for "a well regulated militia, being necessary" for the protection of a state. This was originally made because the makers of the Constitution just had this little tat with England and didn't want a government trying to take over its people. Now this is admirable of government officials to think of its citizens like this and make sure they are protected. However, there is a problem with trying to apply an antiquated idea to modern times. The amendment says you can form a "militia" and not a gang in downtown Los Angeles, California or use your guns for killing people willy-nilly. For the record, nowhere does it even state that a gun should be used in cases of self-defense. Since we are down that road, it also does not say that guns should be used for sport either. Furthermore, if anyone thinks that a militia of little pistols is going to outman the United States military armed with tanks and drones, then we are mistaken.

The need for a militia is just not prevalent in our society. People can say all they want that we have to be protected just in case the government starts to overreach and actually start a war against its people, but if that were to

137

happen, then we will outright lose. Does this warrant a rewrite? Yes. Not just because the biggest military in the world would completely thwart any militia we could form today, but also because this is not enough of a reason to warrant the mass killings, and the everyday shootings that happen in this country. We are a gun country and possibly something that will never change. However, to say that positive gun legislation that will keep our people safer is out of the question is just ridiculous. People are mistaken if they think the constitution supports their beliefs in this. It was not until the Supreme Court "interpreted," but really re-amended the second amendment that we will forever be stuck with guns in this country.

In the court case District of Colombia v. Heller, it was decided that the second amendment:

> "[P]rotects an individual right to possess a firearm unconnected with service in a militia, and to use that arm for traditionally lawful purposes, such as self-defense within the home."[48]

Furthermore, "the right is not unlimited. It is not a right to keep and carry any weapon whatsoever in any manner whatsoever and for whatever purpose."[49] Nowhere in the original amendment does it say anything about an "individual right" to own a gun. Despite people claiming it does. Despite many people also saying it is purposely ambiguous, it is actually pretty clear that the government

---

[48] Wikipedia, "District of Colombia v. Heller," *Wikipedia,* https://en.wikipedia.org/wiki/District_of_Columbia_v._Hel ler, date accessed 29 May 2013

[49] ibid

will not get in the way of people owning a gun in order to maintain a "well regulated militia."

An "interpretation" is explaining the meaning of something else. What the Supreme Court did was add words to the already written and laid out second amendment. Justice Scalia must have been an English major because claiming that the Second Amendment "codified a pre-existing right" is an interpretation of the word "infringed" is ridiculous. It is ridiculous for many reasons, but one of the major ones is the interpretation must be within the context of the entire sentence because the government should not have the right to infringe on people owning a gun to form a "well regulated militia." This is the right they are given – the right to own a gun to form a militia. Why people never read the entire sentence is baffling.

Further defense of an individual right to own a gun is supposedly confirmed by the 1689 English Bill of Rights. However, to anyone who does not know, guns in England are outlawed. Before we go any further in this, let me tell you a story.

There once was a man who went into a school. This man was described as being an oddball and did not really fit into society. Well this man decided to go into a school, with little to no motivation and shoot children who were as young as five years old. Not only did the children's teacher die in this man's mass shooting, but many children died as well. As a result of this horrible tragedy, people were outraged and decided to do something about it so it would not happen again.

This is not a fictional story. Do you know whom I am

talking about? I am sure many people are thinking of the travesty that happened at Sandy Hook Elementary School in Newtown, Connecticut, but that's not the story I am talking about. They are very similar though, so it would have been a good guess. The above story is a brief recap of the events that led to Britain banning personal guns to its citizens. You know Britain right? That place that we proudly based our gun rights laws after?

In 1996, in the Scottish town of Dunblane a man by the name of Thomas Hamilton who was socially awkward like the alleged Newtown shooter Adam Lanza, went into a school and shot 15 children in mere minutes. This was one of the most horrific shootings in the UK and because of that, people were outraged – much like they were in the U.S. However, UK citizens did not stop at outrage, as they wanted action done so that people could not get guns so easily. A petition circulated with 750,000 names on it that demanded action from the government, you know like how 90% of people said they wanted background checks for gun purchases. The Prime Minister at the time, John Major, took it upon himself to look into gun laws, you know like President Obama and Vice President Biden.

And this is where the stories take dramatic turns. In Britain, new legislation was introduced called the Firearms Amendment – oh there's that amendment word again – Act of 1988. This made it mandatory for gun owners to register their guns and it also banned semi-automatic and pump-action weapons. This is what we wanted to do. We sure do copy the British a lot when it comes to our laws. Sadly, just not enough.

Does what they did sound radical? Well it did not stop

there because the legislation then put a ban on all private owned handguns in mainland Britain. An amnesty was held across the UK and thousands of people surrendered guns. I hear the dissenters now, so I will give you some numbers. After this little experiment on gun control, numbers did not change for crimes involving guns. Crimes rose in the 1990s. However, since then there has been a dramatic decline every year thereafter and crimes with handguns dropped 44% in 2010 and 2011.[50]

So just to give a recap: the UK had a massive shooting where a crazed man shoots up a school killing innocent children and a teacher. The people react and guns are banned. In the U.S., a man shoots up a school, killing innocent children and teachers and what happens? Absolutely nothing. Not one piece of legislation is passed to correct the issues or prevent something from happening again. So you want to go back to the Constitution? As stated, nowhere in the Constitution does it justify an individual's right to own a gun. If you want to thank someone for our right to carry firearms, the gun saviors you want to praise is the Supreme Court for interpreting (not so ambiguous) words in favor of a gun country.

Justice Scalia did not go far enough in his interpretation of the word "infringe." His idea is that the government should not breach or do something that would limit the people's right to own a gun would make sense if the second amendment said nothing else other than "the right

---

[50] Peter Wilkinson, "Dunblane: How UK school massacre led to tighter gun control," *CNN*, http://www.cnn.com/2012/12/17/world/europe/dunblane-lessons, 2 June 2013

of the people to keep and bear Arms, shall not be infringed." However, there is a whole part he seemed to leave out that actually precedes everything else. The right people have to own a gun that the government will not infringe upon is to ***own a gun to form a militia***. *In any other case it would be excessive to underline, italicize and put a phrase in bold, but I wanted to make sure no one else missed it.* Much like a British accent, the emphasis was put on the wrong parts of this amendment when the Supreme Court made its decision, completely leaving out other parts.

Can we ever go back now and take the emphasis off of guns in this country and do as Britain did to correct a huge tragedy? In our case we have tragedy after tragedy and we continue to do nothing. This is what I mean when I say that this generation is responsible for inaction. It is not our fault entirely of course because in the heat of the outrage President Obama predicted what was a possibility of happening what later did happen. In December, President Obama claimed, "We know this is a complex issue that stirs deeply held passions and political divides. But the fact that this problem is complex can no longer be an excuse for doing nothing."[51]

And that is what we have done: nothing. No responsible gun laws were passed and the issues have since washed away on capital hill. These memories remain in the

---

[51] Bruce Reed, "A Message from President Obama about Your Petition on Reducing Gun Violence," *Whitehouse.gov*, http://www.whitehouse.gov/blog/2012/12/19/message-president-obama-about-your-petition-reducing-gun-violence, date accessed 3 June 2013

hearts of the victims and their families, as well as many people who still care about making changes to ensure this never happens again. It is almost as if President Obama foretold the future at a December press conference when he stated, "And I would hope that our memories aren't so short that what we saw in Newtown isn't lingering with us, that we don't remain passionate about it only a month later."[52]

Well it has been about five months later (since the time of writing this) and nothing has happened and the story has been taken off the front page.

When did indifference set in on this country that the same constitutional rights given to some should not protect all people? Person A claims they have a right to a gun, but that does not mean person B should then forfeit his or her right to safety. The kids at Sandy Hook Elementary School and the people in movie theatres across the country should not sit in fear that someone with a gun can come in and take their lives. The killer's "right" to own a gun does not supersede someone else's right to life.

It is undeniable that there are responsible gun owners in this country, just as there were responsible gun owners in the UK before they banned guns. The difference is people there were willing to surrender their guns for the greater good. Guns may kill people or people may kill

---

[52] Washington Post, "President Obama's remarks on gun control, fiscal cliff, Dec. 19, 2012 (Transcript)," *Washington Post,* http://articles.washingtonpost.com/2012-12-19/politics/35929025_1_gun-violence-gun-control-fiscal-cliff/6, 3 June 2013

people, but this is a ridiculous debate from the start. It does not matter which kills people. People should not be killed. The fact that there is currently free access to things that are intended to do so is ridiculous. Guns' only purpose is to injure or kill. Any other "weapon" people try to say kills more people than guns like a car or a rock is a baseless argument. Cars were not made with the intentions of killing someone. By the way, in case you say that guns should be for sport, killing an animal is also still killing.

This country is so worried about keeping people from smoking in bars and public places, but it is okay with people walking around with guns. If you thought secondhand smoke was deadly, have a pistol shot in your direction. We are all willing and able to tax smokers until it is economically unfeasible to smoke, so let's do the same with guns. If we are going to settle on the fact that guns are never ever going anywhere, then why shouldn't there be a gun tax and ammunition tax that makes it that much more difficult to have access to guns?

So now that everyone is good and riled up about guns, let's explore the Constitution some more.

This is the third amendment in our constitution:

"No Soldier shall, in time of peace be quartered in any house, without the consent of the Owner, nor in time of war, but in a manner to be prescribed by law."

Is this something we are really concerned with in our day and age? Well apparently it was one of the top three concerns in 1791. Is it truly a worry of ours that our government is going to start allowing soldiers to sleep in our homes uninvited? Some people say well this is actually not the spirit of interpreting this amendment because it is supposed to suggest that government should not intrude on people's private lives and what they do in their homes. If that is true, well then gay marriage should have been passed a long time ago.

Taking this amendment at face value and trying to apply it to today's issues reveals how outdated the document is. Now, that being said if we did a loose (very loose) interpretation of this amendment it would suggest that people have a right to privacy in their homes, secure from government intrusion. That means contraception, abortion, gay marriage, and everything that happens behind closed doors is protected under the constitution.

I can see the dissenters now, so let me heed off any ideas. Do not dare try to put in rape or other unlawful and detestable acts into this group because we are talking about civil rights issues protected by the fourteenth amendment. But let's say someone had the audacity to do so. Do you now see the slipperiness of this sacred document we hold dear to our hearts? You cannot "interpret" it by adding what you want to it.

If it were me, I would much rather a new amendment be made for issues like granting gay marriage than trying to figure out which of these antiquated original 10 applies to a person's right to marry. Gay marriage and immigration were not clear and present issues in 1791 or even on anyone's radar. Clearly, a soldier living in people's bedrooms was the hot button front-page topic of the day – or at least it would have been on the front-page. In the twenty-first century, we have different priorities and different concerns that do not fit into the categories predefined by the Constitution. We run into problems because we continue to try to live by standards set by men who thought slavery was okay. Some issues we face today lie beyond the scope of anything that is currently there. Instead of putting words in the mouths of our founding fathers and trying to figure out what they meant, we can just as easily define what we mean ever so clearly by giving those who deserve certain rights, the rights they currently lack. We are holding ourselves hostage to 18th century ideas.

To save time and a lot of discussion on 4-9, let's just jump straight to ten shall we? In the tenth amendment, it is like the founding fathers gave up and said, "we ran out ideas, but let's cover ourselves." The tenth amendment reads:

> "The powers not delegated to the United States by the Constitution, nor prohibited by it to the States, are reserved to the States respectively, or to the people."[53]

This last amendment says one thing very clearly and that is the makers of this document knew that neither they, nor the things they wrote were infallible. They clearly left things out, and those things that they left out are for the people to decide. Before anyone tries to label me as anti-American or going against the principles of this country by what I laid out in this chapter, I am only using the words of our forefathers. Let us now consider this

---

[53] The Charters of Freedom, "Bill of Rights Transcript Text," *The Charters of Freedom,* http://www.archives.gov/exhibits/charters/bill_of_rights_tr anscript.html, 4 June 2013

last amendment. If immigration reform is not in this original document, which it is not, then it shall be left up to the people. If gay marriage is not in this document, which it is also not, then it shall be left to the people to decide. The people *have* decided and they decided that they want change.

This last amendment leaves democracy open to work, as it should. If we truly lived in a democracy, why is it that we surrender to a few men who sat around a table one day and decided to draft up some rules because they were mad at the English? They created a framework of a nation – not a nation that only works in the frame that they were living in at the time.

Let's review a bit before people's feathers become rustled more than they should have, and nothing gets people more riled up than guns. Let's be very clear that I understand that this is a gun country and there are responsible people who own guns. All I am suggesting is that if we are to dispel the fear, threats, anxiety, and killings in this country, do we need more fuel to the fire. It is not that Obama or the government or anyone else wants to take guns away from you. No one is trying to take rights away. All people like me are saying when we talk about responsible gun control is that we want to preserve the rights of the living so that guns do not become easy ways to take the lives of the innocent. This country does not need more things in it to screw it up. Speaking of which, let's move this conversation to weed.

Either that was the greatest transition or the work of a stoner, but here we are anyway. Now judging a book by its cover anyone would assume that a 22-year-old hippie liberal kid with an agenda would of course be in full support of the legalization of marijuana. In fact this is completely against my thinking. Not all of the kinds in Generation Y are potheads. It is not that I am against the legalization of marijuana because I think people should not be allowed to smoke weed. It is just that I do not think this country needs more junk in it that will allow people to do harm to themselves or make them more inactive. When I say harm themselves, I do not want to enter the whole debate on the dangers of drunk driving versus smoking weed. Forgive me for being frank again, but pitting one stupid act against another does not make one more viable for legalization. There are enough problems this country faces than to help stoners have fun on weekends.

And to liberal friends thinking they are fighting the good fight, no one does anyone any justice lumping issues as gay rights and immigration together with the fight for cannabis. Smoking weed is not a civil right as someone having the right to marry or enter this country legally. There is no discrimination here when potheads cannot buy weed from their dealer. Has the war on drugs worked? No, not at all in fact. That being said, I would like to make an analogy.

Let's say that class starts at 8:00 AM every morning. In a class of thirty kids, everyone agrees that this is the rule and what is expected of the class. Now, let's say that one kid comes in late every morning. Every morning this kid interrupts the class by waltzing in at 8:10. Now the teacher has to send that kid to the principal's office every morning. This routine goes on for months and the kid keeps getting in trouble, only to be let back out to do the same thing the next day. Finally, the principal gets fed up with all the time this kid is wasting and decides to push the class back to accommodate this kid and makes class start at 8:15 AM. The extra five minutes is just for good measure.

Is this scenario, is it fair to the other 29 students who showed up to school each day on time and were responsible that class now starts later in the day? The principal changed the rules to accommodate someone who was breaking the rules to begin with because of course it was not his fault, but the system that failed him. This is exactly what we have done in our war on drugs. We are an "either this or that" country. Either we have a war on drugs, or we have the legalization of drugs. Instead of fixing the problem, the war on drugs has just become a talking point for one side to say how completely ridiculous it is for marijuana to be illegal. Instead of a fair system with fair rules, we have decided to scrap the rules altogether.

Will the dissenters please rise. I see the hands waving in the air saying that everyone benefits from the class starting at 8:15. If the day starts later, and if you are really that passionate, then it is your choice to still show up at 8:00 if you choose. Not everyone has to smoke weed, but those who choose to can benefit from it if they like, right? This would be the same idea in the gun argument. The one thing that I will give stoners in this debate is that weed does nothing to harm other people. If you smoke, it is a personal choice. I am not going to be so overdramatic and say that weed in the hand of the youth is like putting a gun in their hands, but why would we cripple society with more toxic behaviors. In most of my research, the jury is still out on the effects weed has on people. In school when I was young I was told "Don't Do Drugs." It was a simple enough phrase, but now we are saying, "Don't Do Drugs, except…"

We have a responsibility to protect people in this country from themselves. It is the same as the seatbelt law. Weed has far more tar and carcinogens than tobacco, so why would we contribute to the problems in our society by more things that will make us unhealthy.

That all being said, why is this not an issue that Constitution thumpers rally behind, and I mean in support of legalization. People are so worried about their rights being taken away and the fear of government intrusion in their private lives. I have already made it clear that people should be protected from agents that will do us harm. But if you like guns, then why is weed something so abhorrently denied?

From guns to gay marriage to the legalization of marijuana, there are issues in this country that have put us in a stalemate for change. If we think these things are not big enough deals that we do not have productive conversations about them, why are they in the news everyday. People are shot everyday, states vote in favor of gay marriage every few months, and people are being incarcerated for drugs everyday. The system is in place, but from the over two hundred year old document, to the congress that is supposed to act on the will of the people, we have a fundamental problem with the way we govern our nation.

I am a firm believer in democracy and the voices of the people should be heard. This is what makes our country strong and allows us the freedom to say and do what other people in other countries would be killed for saying and doing. None of what was said before was to offend because that undermines the principles I set forth and the spirit of democracy. We have to figure out a way to stop these unjust and senseless killings. We must protect the rights of all those people who live in this country no matter a person's race, creed, sexual orientation, gender, religious beliefs or antireligious beliefs. We must protect this nation from becoming a country of incarceration to one that keeps people out of the streets and out of prison, without merely giving in to the problems we face. Compromise is the greatest of all American principles that this country is founded on, so if we keep to any traditions at all, one where we can sit down at a table and address our current affairs and try to solve them is one institution of this nation that should never die out.

Chapter 13:
A Plea to a Generation

Let me not be the sole voice of the generation (unless any TV networks are looking for that kind of thing – I am still looking at you MSNBC and HBO). I will from now on be entirely serious without the informal jokes because this matter is much too important for our generation to be left to the whims of the older men and women that have all the power to lead us in a wrong direction. There are voices better equipped than mine to say more profound things that I can only imagine, and probably do it with better grammar. If I could achieve anything in this book it is to prove that this generation does not deserve everything that is said about it. We do not deserve the harsh criticisms and we do not deserve the overwhelming praise. There once was a time that good enough was not enough. There once was a time when people would not settle for anything less than absolute justice for everyone. Surely we are all granted "life, liberty and the pursuit of happiness," yet we have been fighting for basic liberties for over 200 years. Our egos are not so large that we will not listen to those that have come before us, but we cannot silence the generation that is ready to speak now.

Young people do not think they know it all. I will repeat this again. Young people are not "know it alls," which is a common quip to dismiss anything that is said from a young person. Just because we have passion behind what we say does not mean we are dismissing other viewpoints. Just because we talk louder does not mean we have nothing to say and we are merely making noise. Just because we talk too much does not mean we have nothing of value to say. We just want to be heard and be considered equals. Unfortunately, older people often hand us microphones, but never turn them on. We are asked our opinions and then told we are too young to have opinions. The only thing to do with a muted microphone is to yell. Loudness is not equivalent to being right, but sometimes it is the only way we can be heard. I will be the first to say I do not know everything and nor would I want to. If I did that would mean I would stop learning and growing. I can only share my ideas and thoughts with other people to hopefully enter a discourse that has been ongoing for much longer than I have been alive.

I put my humble opinions in this book (although sometimes they probably did not read as humble) because this generation has much to gain if it is willing to become more than the social media generation. It also has much to lose because the deck really is stacked against us. We are not victims by any means, but we are a group of people who must try and solve the problems generations before ours have either ignored or created. In order to do this, we are going to have to play along and join in their game. The odds are against us, but like so many startup companies created by young people that fail, we cannot just create our own civilizations and hope for coexistence. We will have to integrate into the ranks and demand a place where we are denied one.

This generation faces problems that are both new and old. No generation of young people has seen the level of transparency and global awareness that we have. This generation – as every other before it knew, and as every new generation to come will know - we are living in a special time to shape the future for how we see fit. There will be dissenters. There will be people who think there is nothing wrong with the direction that this generation is taking. There will be people who think that this generation is already doing bigger and better things than those before us. However, until we have complete equality and the hope for complete equality is no longer considered a naïve notion, we will always have something to fight for in this country. Whether it is racial discrimination, age discrimination, sexism, religious bias, classism or whatever –ism that exists in this country, injustice is something we should not tolerate. All the problems of this generation might not be solved in this generation and in our efforts to fix some problems, we might create a few of our own. When that time comes I would expect other young people to be passionate and driven enough to want to do something about it. However, we are not there yet. We are in a place where we are just waiting to see if something happens. Everyone is watching everyone else waiting to see if someone is going to make the first move. We all know there are problems in this country and we acknowledge that someone must do something about it. Why is it not you?

Even if this starts with a simple question, we have to understand that change is not going to happen without young people finding their voices. I used to like the idea that Generation Y was called that because we were the "why" generation. There was this idea that we refused to settle for an answer that we are given and we will constantly question why things are the way they are. The word "why" is a powerful one because, as you can often learn talking to a small child, it can be asked in response to almost any statement, and it still warrants an answer.

The government is corrupt. Why?
The sky is blue. Why?
I am hungry. Why?
Corporate America is full of greedy individuals. Why?
Students cannot find jobs once they leave college. Why?
This generation does not ask enough questions. Why?

Each of those statements, no matter how ridiculous, philosophical, or mundane completely gets called into question when you ask "why?" Forget Facebook, Twitter, Tubmlr, YouTube, social media, cell phones, tablets and technology. The most powerful weapon this generation has is to question everything. People say that we should "question authority" all the time, but they never say how. They never say with what. Questioning people for the sake of it can be an upsetting experience for the person being barraged with questions, but do you know what is a great question to follow up with once you see a sign of their anger? Why? Why are you getting angry? If people can make statements they must have justification for what they say. They must be held responsible and be accountable for what comes out of their mouth, or what is said in a forum online. Without this, we are surrendering our greatest power, and that is to ask questions that demand an answer.

We cannot spread lies without expecting someone to want to know the validity of a given statement. We cannot elect people without knowing their actual stances on issues. We cannot trust our lives with other people who are supposed to have our best interests at heart without understanding their principles first. Someone cannot manage us at work without us understanding his or her reasoning for giving an order. We cannot manage someone without having justifications for what we tell

155

someone to do. All of this depends on us to have a voice and merely ask "why?" Why are things the way they are? Why are we not doing anything about it? Is a single word going to change a culture, which will then change the world? Would I be naïve to think so? Of course I would be foolish to think that a mass of young people challenging an idea to seek the change they desire is going to work.

Tell the young people in the Deep South who fought for civil rights that they were foolish for dying for a right to be treated as equals. Tell the young people who joined the marches and protests to support civil rights for everyone that they were naïve. Tell the young Americans we know as "hippies" they were idiotic for standing up against unjust wars and senseless killings overseas. Tell the nineteen-year-old woman who changes the minds of her once ignorant parents about the other woman she loves that she is herself ignorant. Tell the young mixed race couple who bravely walk down the street as they silence bigots who do not believe in interracial marriage that they are foolish. Tell the children of immigrant parents who fight for their families to be accepted in this country that they are imprudent. Tell young people all over the world that they do not have a voice and everything they have to say simply does not matter.

There is power in this generation, just as there was in the past. The only difference is it is in fragments spread out all over the country and there is not a collective voice that fights for the issues of every young person. We have seen what the power of young voters can do. They can truly leave an impact on this political process and make a statement about the direction of this country. This is not enough, as the need for change does not die on election nights.

The title of this chapter says that this is a plea to a generation, and not to over-generalize but this is not just a plea to young people. This is an open plea to anyone and everyone who has a voice and is seeking to bring about change this country has been desperate for since the founders first created a nation. I criticized the Constitution a bit in this book, but a more perfect union is something that we will always strive for, and when I talk about the importance of words, think about how clever it was to include the word "more" in this phrase: "a *more* perfect union." When it comes to this country, perfection is fluid and never static. Rarely do you hear about something being better than perfect, but the reason this is so prevalent is because we cannot be satisfied with the idea of perfection we are living in today. We might be perfect as a union, which is debatable, but as a people we can definitively and continually improve.

I think about the future of this country not just for myself, but the children, my nieces and nephews, my own future children that will have to grow up and deal with the same greed, corruption, bigotry, racism, sexism, ageism, intolerance, and hatred that exists today, I become saddened that a nation cannot put aside petty differences for the sake of an even more perfect country. The more I grow up and start to leave adolescence behind, the more naïve I hope I become. I would hate to be jaded by the experiences I have had to only teach future generations that they will never have it better than I did. This is the responsibility and burden that this generation has. This is the burden that every generation has had and will have for many years to come. If we do nothing to make the lives of younger people easier and safer, we have failed them and ourselves. This is not a guilt trip because there is nothing to feel guilty about, yet. If we choose to do nothing about the injustices that still exist in this country then we should feel responsible. Until that time comes we have a choice to make. We can allow this generation to come to a close, only to have the next named generation Z try its hand at what we did not accomplish. Or we can define ourselves and make a lasting impression on this world that will outlive Generation Y.

Well, why not?

www.ingramcontent.com/pod-product-compliance
Lightning Source LLC
Chambersburg PA
CBHW070653290526
45790CB00001B/299